Nutrition for "Normal People"

John Core

Copyright © 2024 John Core
All rights reserved.
ISBN:
9798333655073

Staten House

CillAid
Publications

For Roisin,
Cillian & Aidan

CONTENTS

Acknowledgments i
Introduction ix

1	WHAT IS FOOD?	1
2	WHAT IS "NORMAL"?	9
3	OUR SEDENTARY WORLD	15
4	MACRONUTRIENTS; PROTEIN	23
5	MACRONUTRIENTS; FATS	31
6	MACRONUTRIENTS; CARBOHYDRATES	39
7	FIBRE	49
8	THE 7/30 RULE	59
9	THE MEDITERRANEAN DIET	67
10	MOOD FOOD	75
11	HYDRATION AND DRINKS	83
12	FERMENTED FOODS	93
13	GUT HEALTH	107
14	POOP!	121
15	WEIGHT MANAGEMENT	129
16	FASTING	137
17	SLEEP	145
18	HOW TO EAT	153
19	POLYPHENOLS	163
20	SAVVY SHOPPING AND CHOOSING YOUR FOODS	169
21	FOOD LABELS	195
22	A ROUGH GUIDE TO EATING OVER A "NORMAL" WEEK	203
23	INDULGENCES	215

ACKNOWLEDGMENTS

First and foremost, I extend my deepest gratitude to my wife, Roisin. Your support of my career, especially during the challenging times when our children were born, has been invaluable. Your ability to pick up the slack and allowing me to finish my academic studies while working long hours is something I will always be grateful for.

I would also like to express my heartfelt thanks to Annette Sweeney at TU Dublin. Annette, your dedication to upskilling myself and many other chefs in the field of applied culinary nutrition has been extraordinary. Your talent in making such a complex subject accessible to students, many of whom, like me, have little academic background, is truly remarkable.

A special thanks to my employer, Sodexo Ireland, for providing me with the platform and resources to advance my career in the emerging field of culinary nutrition. Your support and the freedom you have given me to explore and implement new ideas within our business have been pivotal in allowing me to support our clients effectively.

I want to honour the memory of the late Paula Mee. Paula's influence on my academic journey was profound. Although not formally appointed as my applied research supervisor, Paula provided support and encouraged me to publish my work. For this I will always be grateful.

Lastly, to Mam and Dad, thanks for everything.

INTRODUCTION

This book offers a general overview of nutrition, touching lightly on the themes I frequently encounter in my culinary nutrition work. The aim of this piece of work is to address the most common questions I've encountered during the seminars and webinars I have delivered over the years; all asked by "Normal People". While I haven't spent extensive time in a lab researching every aspect of nutrition, and I am not a registered dietitian qualified to advise on medical conditions, my qualifications come from a different place. I have worked in the culinary field from a young age, both as a chef and in overseeing large-scale catering operations, primarily for sedentary people. The nutrition needs of these people have been the focus of my academic studies and professional career since I graduated with an MSc in Applied Culinary Nutrition in 2020.

In my role, overseeing food offerings and delivering seminars and webinars to large audiences, I need to be well-versed in all aspects of nutrition to ensure a healthy food offering and to answer client and customer queries effectively. What I believe sets me apart in writing this guidance is that I come from the perspective of a "normal" person.

Growing up in the 80s with a typical diet of that generation, I never encountered foods like bell peppers or courgettes until I started working in professional kitchens at the age of 15. Over the years, I have worked in various kitchens worldwide with many chefs of many nationalities, expanding my culinary horizons. My palate has broadened significantly, and my diet now is very different from before I undertook my academic studies and professional work in culinary nutrition. However, the "normal" diet, which often includes heavily processed foods, still occasionally features in my food choices, albeit in a very small way.

I have a deep love for all types of food, and cooking and eating are central to my daily life. I feel equally at home in a health-focused food outlet, a fine dining restaurant, or a gourmet burger bar. While franchised fast food is probably my least favourite, I find the trend of ethnic takeaway food to be a positive and exciting addition to high street offerings. However, like fast food, most takeaways are not made with nutrition as their primary focus. Their priority tends to be hyper palatable food and cost control, which is fine if they are treated as occasional indulgences. If it wasn't for my knowledge in the culinary nutrition space my inner glutton would have me very obese man, so the guidance in this book works for me as I hope it would for my readers.

I think everyone should have a base knowledge of nutrition. Everyone should know how to make good food decisions and know that the more exciting you make your food by different ingredients and flavours the better it will be for you. When it comes to nutrition, we are overwhelmed with information but often lack true knowledge. Social media is flooded with conflicting advice, especially from influencers who may not fully understand what constitutes a healthy diet. These influencers often gain followers by promoting so-called "silver bullets" of healthy eating, but the reality is, there is no one-size-fits-all solution. Consuming any single food or food group exclusively is not healthy. Nutrition is incredibly complex, involving a multitude of chemicals and compounds in food, which our bodies metabolise through a sophisticated process of mechanical digestion, enzymes, and internal chemistry. It's highly unlikely that an attractive person on Instagram knows every factor affecting your body's energy metabolism when they advise you to drastically restrict your diet to a single food, food group, or worse, a supplement or food-like powder as your main source of calories.

This book is structured so that each chapter reads like an article, allowing you to dip in and out of chapters without needing to read it from start to finish. If you really can't be bothered to read the chapters, I have even summarized the key points at the end of most of them to make it really user friendly to get the points. This format leads to a significant amount of repetition, reflecting the recurring themes in nutrition. The same foods that are good for sustainably managing weight are also beneficial for gut health, concentration, and a host of other health benefits.

Nutrition can seem vastly complex due to the intricate chemistry of food and the complexity of the biological systems that process it. However, it is also fundamentally simple:

- Learn how to cook so you are in full control of what goes into your food.
- Eat a balanced diet, primarily composed of whole plant foods, good quality proteins, and healthy fats, most of which should be unsaturated and sourced responsibly.
- Choose foods that don't have labels listing numerous unrecognisable ingredients.
- Follow this approach most of the time, but also allow yourself the occasional indulgence in the treats you enjoy so you are not denying yourself anything.
- That's essentially it.

My perspective on nutrition comes from my background as a chef. Although I have conducted extensive academic research in this field, I gravitate towards aspects of nutrition that feel natural. Without needing to read this entire book, my advice is as simple as stated above; as much as possible, eat whole foods, with the majority being plants from a diverse range of sources. Avoid ultra-processed foods, though they are hard to avoid entirely, so keep them to a minimum. Eat lean meats and high-quality dairy, preferably from local sources. If you follow a plant-based diet, ensure you research to get the right combination of plants to meet your nutritional needs. Keep refined starches to a minimum unless you need quick energy for physical activities. Enjoy your food and flavour it with herbs, spices, and aromatics from various cuisines; these colours and flavours will benefit your health. Keep alcohol consumption to a minimum. Most importantly, don't let your diet define you; indulge occasionally, so long as these indulgences are less than twenty percent of your food choices.

As I approach nutrition from a culinary perspective, I rely on academic research by those more qualified in this field. If, after reading this book, you want to explore further and consider works by experts such as Giulia Enders, Tim Spector, Joanna McMillan, Sarah Keogh, Chris van Tulleken, and Will Bulsiewicz. They all communicate their findings in a way that is accessible to the "normal" person.

Finally, a disclaimer: the guidance in this book is based on my opinions and should not replace professional medical advice. Always consult a healthcare professional before starting any new dietary supplement or making significant dietary changes. However, you don't need to consult anyone if you want to cut junk food out of your diet and start eating better-quality foods and more fruits and vegetables. You have my full permission to do that.

CHAPTER 1
WHAT IS FOOD?

Over the past few years, it has been my job to move past my training as a chef and food service provider to look at the broader impact of food on our health, society, and the environment. Most people look at the food they eat as either a reward, fuel, or they deep dive into its weight management properties. The truth is most people think that anything they can eat is food, which is not always the case, so the question must be asked, what is food?

Food, in its most basic definition, is any substance consumed to provide nutritional support for the body. It usually consists of essential nutrients, such as carbohydrates, fats, proteins, vitamins, and minerals, which are necessary for maintaining health and sustaining life. Traditionally, food has been derived from plants and animals, including fruits, vegetables, grains, meat, and dairy. These whole foods, as they are often called, are minimally processed, and retain most of their natural nutrients and fibre.

In contrast, our modern diet has increasingly incorporated many edible food-like substances. These products, while edible and often delicious, differ significantly from traditional whole foods. They are typically highly processed, containing numerous additives, preservatives, artificial flavours, and sweeteners. Examples include soft drinks, crisps, sugary cereals, and ready-made meals.

Food has been a pivotal factor in human evolution over the past million years. The advent of cooking significantly impacted our development. As we began to cook, the nutrients within the food became more easily absorbed, contributing to the enlargement of our brains. Today, a significant portion of our brain is dedicated to our senses, particularly sight, taste, smell, and even sound, all of which profoundly affect how we perceive our food and the choices we make. Food producers are aware of this and use this knowledge to market their products and adults and children.

Like most parents, I am very aware of how young children can be particularly picky eaters. However, in the first couple of years of life, children are highly receptive to new foods, instantly putting any new foods (and often non-food objects) in their mouth. This openness allows young children to adapt to and accept a wider range of foods, which will inevitably dwindle over time as they start to reject newer food items like green vegetables. This evolutionary caution to new food means that, from early childhood, children tend to be cautious of potentially dangerous bitter or sharp-tasting foods while showing a preference for sweet, fatty, and savoury foods, which we evolved to recognise as energy rich.

From childhood our perception of food is significantly affected by its smell, texture, colour, and shape. These sensory attributes influence how we taste different foods. Our brains dedicate a significant portion to visualising food, much more than to tasting. The attractiveness of brightly coloured fruits, such as red strawberries, green apples, and purple grapes, is rooted in our evolutionary history. These colours signal high sugar content, promising sweetness and energy. Plants have evolved to enhance their fruits' appeal to ensure animals consume the fruits and scatter the seeds elsewhere. Humans then took charge of the process, and by cross-pollinating and selectively breeding plants, we now have shelves in the supermarket filled with fruits and vegetables that are far removed from their original natural iteration many generations ago. These modern fruits and vegetables are bigger, sweeter, brighter, more colourful, and more pest and disease resistant than their original ancestors. Many supermarket fruits and vegetables can be a couple of months or even a year old. They are picked unripe, stored, and then chemically ripened. All to ensure they are the perfect size and colour to entice us to buy them.

Our food has shaped us as much as we have shaped it. Our evolutionary journey with food has not only influenced our biological development but also our sensory perceptions and cultural practices. Understanding this intricate relationship can help us make better dietary choices and appreciate the profound role food plays in our lives.

Humans possess an extraordinary ability to discern a wide array of food flavours due to our smell receptors. These hundreds of receptors capture thousands of natural chemicals, enabling us to distinguish a vast amount of aroma combinations. Our brain saves these as very powerful memories, which is why the smell of the sea might instantly make you think of a childhood trip to the beach, or a certain food smell might make you think instantly of the parent or grandparent who used to make it for you. This significantly large part of the brain is crucial for anticipating food. We are remarkably sensitive to different smells. The anticipation of eating, even just thinking about food, stimulates our digestive system and appetite hormones, triggering stomach acid release. When we eat, our taste and smell receptors are activated, enriching the flavour experience. Saliva, containing various enzymes, aids in this process. The shape and texture of food, like the rounded or angular cuts of an apple, or the shape of a piece of chocolate, also influence our perception of taste.

Our sensory evaluation of food is often misleading, with our brains prioritising sight and taste over other senses. Taste receptors distributed across the tongue detect multiple flavours, and genetic variations in these receptors explain differences in taste preferences, such as why some people perceive coriander to taste like soap. Sound also affects our perception of food, albeit to a lesser extent. This is evident when we eat an apple or crisps and hear the satisfying crunch.

Ultra-processed foods (UPFs) are engineered to be highly appealing by combining fat, salt, and sugar, which stimulate the pleasure centres in the brain. This triggers the release of dopamine, a feel-good neurochemical, overriding our natural fullness signals. The combination of fat, sugar, salt, and a crunchy texture transforms basic ingredients with little to no nutritional benefit into highly addictive foods. The addition of flavour enhancers, artificial sweeteners, and other chemicals further intensifies this brain response, disrupting our hunger hormones and making it hard for us to feel satisfied in the long term.

Unlike natural foods, UPFs are uniquely addictive, leading to overconsumption and poor nutrition which is a significant concern for children growing up on these foods.
It is well known that people who consume plant-based diets are generally healthier and have fewer heart health issues than those who consume a lot of meat and dairy. Fish consumption, especially fatty fish like mackerel and salmon, is also considered healthy. On the other hand, meat consumption, particularly red and processed meat, is associated with heart disease, some cancers, and overall mortality. This is especially true for low-quality meats commonly found in ultra-processed foods and ready meals.

In Ireland and the UK, the recommendation is to consume more than five servings of fruits and vegetables daily as the pillar of a healthy diet. Really this is just scratching the surface as we need to be heavily promoting potential benefits of a diverse plant-based diet and the real number of fruit and vegetable portions we need to eat daily is probably over seven. We need to explore the wide variety of edible plants, beyond just their fibre and calorie content, to understand what makes some plants healthier than others and the benefits of consuming a plant in huge variety rather than just promoting five or more portions a day.

Plants contain a huge number of compounds and chemicals, many of which remain unresearched. These phytochemicals help plants sustain themselves, reproduce, and defend against threats. Polyphenols in plants protect against sun damage and act as deterrents against predators and parasites. Some polyphenols are beneficial in small amounts but toxic in excess, like nicotine, caffeine, and cyanide found in fruit seeds. Different plant parts have varied roles and chemical compositions. Young sprouts and leaves, rich in protective polyphenols, are often used as flavourful herbs. Other parts of the plants like the flesh and roots can be dried and powdered and used as spices such as chilli and turmeric.
The advice to "Eat the Rainbow" highlights the importance of consuming a variety of colourful fruits and vegetables, each offering unique health benefits due to their unique polyphenols giving different plants, different colours. However, it's crucial to consume these foods in their natural, whole form rather than as processed products.

While certain nutrients are marketed for specific health benefits, the true advantage of healthy eating lies in the combination of various plant chemicals interacting with our gut microbiome. Our bodies have innate mechanisms for disease prevention, aging, and cancer defence, which rely on a healthy microbiome and essential nutrients. As we age, maintaining these defences becomes more challenging, underscoring the importance of a balanced, plant-rich diet.

My definition of unhealthy foods is probably foods that don't benefit our biology. Fast-absorbing foods in the small intestine, resulting in fats and sugars entering the bloodstream quickly and leaving nothing for the colon, are also unhealthy. These include many UPFs, causing sugar and fat spikes, overeating, and inflammation. UPFs are typically convenient, hyper-palatable, and with long shelf lives. UPFs are characterised by their complex chemical mixtures and lack of resemblance to whole foods. To identify UPFs, check for ingredients rarely used in kitchens or various additives aimed at enhancing palatability. UPFs are linked to overeating and obesity. They are less satiating than whole foods and can upset the body's natural satiety signals (feelings of fullness). These foods make up over half of the calories in the UK and US diets with Ireland very close behind as we tend to be with most trends seen in the western world. UPFs usually contain low levels of quality protein, fibre, and polyphenols. Chemicals in UPFs disrupt our gut microbes and make these foods addictive. The lack of chewing and increased eating speed associated with UPFs may also affect these fullness signals because you have eaten them in their entirety so quickly before you can start to feel full.

UPFs are associated to be prevalent in countries with high obesity rates like the US, UK, Canada, and Australia. Reducing UPFs in diets, particularly in children, could significantly reduce obesity rates. In contrast, countries like Portugal and Italy, where UPFs constitute a small portion of the diet, show lower obesity rates and healthier populations.
The choices we make about the food we consume have far-reaching impacts that extend beyond our personal health to the health of our planet. The environmental issues we face today, such as climate change, pollution, and biodiversity loss, are increasingly connected to our dietary habits.

Our current food production systems contribute significantly to these environmental problems. For instance, deforestation, often driven by the need for agricultural land, results in the loss of biodiversity and the release of carbon stored in trees into the atmosphere, exacerbating climate change. The production of certain foods, particularly meat, is a major driver of deforestation in regions like the Amazon rainforest. The intensive agriculture industry is a substantial source of greenhouse gas emissions. Livestock farming alone accounts for a significant portion of methane emissions, a potent greenhouse gas. The use of synthetic fertilisers and pesticides in crop production also contributes to pollution and the degradation of ecosystems,

Another pressing issue is plastic packaging. Much of the food we purchase comes in plastic, which often ends up in landfills or the ocean, where it can harm marine life and ecosystems. Reducing plastic use in food packaging is crucial for mitigating this form of pollution.

Given these environmental challenges, our dietary choices can make a significant difference. **Each food choice we make is essentially a decision that affects our future health and acts as a vote for how that food is produced.** When we choose sustainably sourced, organic, or plant-based foods, we support farming practices that are less harmful to the environment. For instance, buying organic produce encourages farming that avoids synthetic chemicals and promotes biodiversity.

Similarly, every euro spent on food is an investment in the food system that delivers that food to your table. By spending money on products from companies that prioritise sustainability, we can drive demand for more environmentally friendly practices. This economic support helps these businesses grow and encourages others to adopt similar practices.

Consumers have the power to influence food production systems through their purchasing decisions. For example, choosing locally produced food reduces the carbon footprint associated with transportation. Opting for seasonal produce can decrease the energy required for growing and storing food out of season. Reducing meat consumption and increasing plant-based foods in our diets can lower the demand for resource-intensive livestock farming. By being mindful of where our food comes from and how it is produced, we can contribute to a more sustainable food system. This conscious approach not only benefits our health, by often leading to the consumption of fresher and more nutritious foods, but also supports the health of our planet by reducing the environmental impact of our diets.

CHAPTER 2
WHAT IS "NORMAL"?

In our modern Irish society, the average lifestyle has evolved significantly, especially when compared to that of previous generations. This transformation is largely influenced by technological advancements, changes in work, and the increasing digitisation of daily activities.

A typical working day for many people involves a 9-to-5 job, often in an office environment. Unlike the physically demanding jobs of past generations, which required substantial manual labour, many modern jobs are sedentary. This shift from physical to more mental tasks has led to a decrease in the overall energy expenditure of the average worker. While our parents and grandparents might have spent their days engaged in farming, construction, or other physically intensive activities, today's workforce is more likely to be found sitting at a desk.

The sedentary nature of modern jobs means that most people spend a considerable part of their day sitting. This is further compounded by the time spent commuting. Whether stuck in traffic in a car or sitting on public transport, the average commuter experiences extended periods of inactivity. This daily routine of prolonged sitting contributes to various health issues, including poor posture, back pain, and increased risk of chronic diseases such as heart disease and diabetes. With the demanding work schedules and long commutes, finding time for exercise has become increasingly challenging. Despite the well-known benefits of regular physical activity, many people struggle to incorporate it into their daily routines. This lack of exercise can lead to weight gain, muscle loss, and a general decline in physical fitness, which can have long-term implications for overall health and wellbeing.

A significant portion of our day is now spent in front of digital screens. At work, computers are essential tools for completing tasks, while at home, many unwind by watching TV or browsing the internet on their mobile devices. This pervasive presence of digital screens has not only changed how we work and relax but also how we interact with the world around us. Excessive screen time is linked to eye strain, poor sleep quality, and decreased physical activity, as it often replaces more active forms of entertainment and socialisation.

Modern eating habits have drastically changed, and this shift is significantly influenced by convenience and the fast pace of life.

Many people consume refined and processed foods regularly. These foods, which include items like white bread, sugary cereals, and packaged snacks, are most likely low in essential nutrients and high in added sugars, unhealthy fats, and sodium. The convenience and shelf-life of these products make them a popular choice, despite their negative impact on health. Consuming such foods can lead to various health issues, including obesity, diabetes, and cardiovascular diseases.

Breakfast is often seen as the most important meal of the day, yet many people opt for quick and easy options like cereal or toast. Most commercially available cereals are high in sugar and low in fibre and protein, leading to a quick spike in blood sugar levels followed by a crash, which can affect energy and concentration throughout the morning. Toast, especially when made with white bread and topped with sugary spreads, offers little nutritional value, and can contribute to poor diet quality.

For lunch, sandwiches and wraps are common choices due to their portability and ease of preparation. While these can be healthy options if made with whole-grain bread, lean proteins, and plenty of vegetables, they often contain processed meats, high-fat spreads, and refined grains. These ingredients can add unnecessary calories and unhealthy fats to the diet, and they might lack sufficient nutrients like fibre, vitamins, and minerals. These are often consumed in large portions and not balanced with the right proportion of vegetables and proteins. Takeaway dinners, which are increasingly popular, tend to be high in unhealthy fats, sugars, and sodium. Regularly consuming these meals can lead to weight gain and other health issues due to their high calorie and low nutrient content.

Weekends often involve dining out, which can lead to the consumption of large portions and high-calorie foods. Restaurants and pubs frequently serve meals rich in fats, sugars, and salts. Additionally, weekends are a common time for higher alcohol consumption. Alcoholic drinks are calorie-dense and can contribute to weight gain and liver problems when consumed excessively. The social aspect of eating out and drinking can also encourage overindulgence.

Fast food franchises are popular for their convenience and low cost. However, the foods offered by these establishments are typically high in calories, unhealthy fats, sugars, and sodium. The industrialised food production systems used in these franchises prioritise cost and efficiency over nutritional value. Regular consumption of fast food is linked to obesity, heart disease, and other chronic health conditions due to its poor nutritional profile.

Supermarkets are the primary source of food for most people. While they offer a wide variety of fresh produce, lean meats, and whole grains, they also stock an abundance of processed and convenience foods. Marketing and product placement often lead consumers to choose less healthy options. The prevalence of ready-made meals, sugary snacks, and processed foods can make it challenging to maintain a balanced diet.

Marketing and advertising play a significant role in shaping food choices. Companies spend vast amounts of money on advertising campaigns that often target children and adolescents. These advertisements typically promote processed and sugary foods with enticing visuals and catchy slogans. The influence of such marketing can lead to unhealthy eating habits from a young age, as people are persuaded to choose these advertised products over healthier alternatives. The appeal of convenience foods, often highlighted in these ads, further cements their place in the daily diet.

Cultural and social factors are powerful determinants of dietary habits. Food is deeply intertwined with cultural identity, traditions, and social interactions. Different cultures have distinct cuisines and food practices, which influence what people eat and how they eat it. Social gatherings, family traditions, and communal meals often revolve around specific foods, which can range from healthy to unhealthy. Societal norms and peer influences can affect your food choices, encouraging conformity to prevalent eating patterns, whether beneficial or detrimental.

Economic factors significantly impact food choices. In many cases, healthier food options, such as fresh fruits and vegetables, lean meats, and whole grains, are more expensive than processed and refined foods. People with limited financial resources may opt for cheaper, calorie-dense foods that provide immediate satisfaction but lack nutritional value. Urban environments and areas with limited access to affordable and nutritious food, further exacerbate this issue, making it challenging for people in these regions to maintain a healthy diet. Economic constraints often lead to a reliance on convenience foods, which are more affordable and accessible but less healthy.

The shift from physically demanding jobs to more sedentary office work has led to a decrease in overall physical activity, contributing to various health issues such as poor posture, back pain, and an increased risk of chronic diseases. Additionally, the prevalence of prolonged screen time and convenience-driven eating habits has further exacerbated these health concerns. I understand this well because I embody the definition of 'normal' in today's context. I regularly spend four hours a day in the car or more on long commutes for work.

My job can cause me to live in a very sedentary way, as it involves online meetings, seminars, webinars, and writing nutrition pieces. Another aspect I reflect on in this area, is that growing up in Dublin in the 80s, processed foods were the norm and, in many cases, even desirable as products like frozen pizzas became available in supermarkets. Adverts on the TV would advertise new ready meals and frozen desserts, and these became aspirational food that children would pester their parents for.

Reflecting on Paul Howard's character, Ross O'Carroll Kelly, he writes something in one of the early books along the lines of, "I'm as working class as curry chips, easy singles, and a loan from the credit union." I find this quote resonant for two reasons: firstly, it reflects my own working-class background, and secondly, it highlights how food serves as a marker of identity. Food is the great unifier; everyone eats, the food choices you make is an identifier of class and your place in society. Sadly, more and more people are consuming foods that do not nourish them but instead make them sick and they make these decisions based on their habits, upbringing and socio-economic background.

In my work in culinary nutrition, I see the scientific evidence daily for why these dietary habits are harmful. This knowledge has significantly influenced my own diet, yet I still occasionally choose to eat the foods I grew up with, like hotdogs, ramen noodle packets, and ultra-processed snacks such as Pringles. These foods are comforting and delicious to me, though I am acutely aware they are not truly food, which is why they remain an occasional treat.

To address these challenges, promoting awareness about the importance of regular physical activity and balanced diets is essential. Encouraging healthier eating habits, such as opting for whole grains, lean proteins, and plenty of vegetables, can help mitigate the negative impact of modern dietary trends. Additionally, finding ways to incorporate more physical activity into daily routines, despite the demands of modern work schedules, is crucial for improving overall health and wellbeing.

By making conscious choices to prioritise physical activity and healthy eating, you can counteract the negative effects of a sedentary lifestyle and poor dietary habits, leading to better long-term health outcomes.

CHAPTER 3
OUR SEDENTARY WORLD

In today's technology-driven world, the way we live, eat, and move has drastically changed from what our bodies are naturally designed for.

Our ancestors led a life that was inherently active. They walked, ran, hunted, and gathered - all activities that required significant physical exertion. This constant movement wasn't just a choice but a necessity for survival. In stark contrast, the modern lifestyle is predominantly sedentary. We have engineered physical activity out of our lives with advancements like cars, lifts, escalators, and desk jobs. For me and many like me this sedentary working day has led to a host of health issues, as our bodies are genetically programmed to be active.

The dietary habits of our hunter-gatherer ancestors were dictated by availability and necessity. Their diets were diverse, seasonal, and unprocessed, in stark contrast to the modern diet, which is often calorie-dense, nutrient-poor, and laden with processed foods. This dramatic shift in dietary patterns has led to an increase in diseases like obesity, diabetes, and heart disease.

Fibre for sedentary people

Fibre, found in plant-based foods, is a complex carbohydrate that the body finds harder to digest. This indigestibility is precisely what gives fibre its health benefits. There are two types of fibre – soluble and insoluble – both of which play crucial roles in our diet.

Some Foods High in Soluble Fibre:

- Oats
- Apples
- Oranges
- Carrots
- Barley
- Lentils
- Beans (such as black beans and kidney beans)
- Sweet potatoes
- Peas

Some Foods High in Insoluble Fibre:

- Whole wheat bread
- Brown rice
- Nuts (such as almonds and walnuts)
- Seeds (such as flaxseeds and sunflower seeds)
- Green beans
- Potatoes (with skin)
- Cauliflower
- Broccoli
- Bran cereal
- Popcorn

One of the most significant benefits of a high fibre diet is its impact on satiety (felling of fullness). Fibre adds bulk to the diet without adding calories, helping you feel fuller for longer after eating. This prolonged feeling of fullness can help reduce overall calorie intake, an essential factor in weight management. In a sedentary lifestyle where calorie expenditure is low, consuming foods that help manage hunger can be a crucial strategy in preventing weight gain.

Foods high in fibre generally require more chewing, which not only slows down the eating process, giving your body time to recognise fullness but also typically means they are less energy dense. This is beneficial for those leading a sedentary lifestyle as it helps manage calorie intake more effectively.

Consuming fewer calories while feeling satisfied is a practical approach to counteract the limited physical activity that characterizes modern life.

Beyond satiety and calorie control, a high fibre diet has other health benefits that are particularly relevant in the context of sedentary lifestyles. Fibre aids in slowing the absorption of sugar, helping to control blood sugar levels. It also plays a role in lowering cholesterol levels, contributing to heart health.

To mimic the diverse, unprocessed diet of our ancestors and see the benefits of a high fibre intake, incorporating a variety of fibre-rich foods is essential. Fruits, vegetables, whole grains, legumes, nuts, and seeds are excellent sources of fibre. These foods not only provide fibre but also a wide range of nutrients that can help counteract the negative effects of a sedentary lifestyle and a diet high in processed foods.

Why Exercise?

Exercise, while a stressor on the body, initiates a cascade of beneficial responses that enhance our physical and mental health. When we engage in physical activity, our body activates its intrinsic repair and maintenance systems. This includes the production of antioxidants, which combat oxidative stress, and enzymes that repair DNA and protein damage. These physiological responses are crucial for reducing the risk of chronic diseases and promoting longevity.

Our evolutionary history has hardwired us for movement. From hunting and gathering to farming and now, in some cases, leading more sedentary lifestyles, our bodies thrive on being active. Regular physical activity is crucial for stimulating health-promoting mechanisms, including the activation of components of the immune system like natural killer cells, which play a role in cancer prevention.

For exercise to be a sustainable part of your lifestyle, it should be both enjoyable and socially engaging. Incorporating fun activities, such as sports, dancing, and social walks, can transform exercise from a chore into a normal part of the day.

A balanced exercise regimen should include a mix of moderate and vigorous activities, along with strength training. This approach ensures that all aspects of fitness—cardiovascular health, muscle strength, and endurance—are addressed. It's essential to note that while extreme forms of exercise, such as marathon running, can be driven by personal goals, they are not necessary for maintaining health. The key is consistency and finding a routine that fits your lifestyle and preferences.

Creating routines can significantly enhance the likelihood of maintaining a regular exercise regimen. Simple strategies, such as going for a walk in the morning or performing body-weight exercises during short breaks, can seamlessly integrate physical activity into daily life. A good rule of thumb is that all your activities should have you active for half an hour, if it's a jog or circuit training class or weights session then 3 times a week is a good starting point. If it's less intense exercise like a good walk etc then you should up this to 5 days a week. These routines ensure that exercise becomes a non-negotiable part of the day, like eating or sleeping.

Aging and Activity

It's a common belief today that aging is synonymous with a decline in physical activity. The emergence of sedentary lifestyles has fostered an aversion to exercise, seen as an unnecessary exertion of energy rather than a beneficial and enjoyable part of daily routines.

However, this hasn't always been the case, and it certainly shouldn't be. Historically, the elderly of the community were not only relied on for their wisdom but were also integral to the physical fabric of their communities. They engaged in daily tasks, contributed to communal work, and were active participants in society.

In many traditional societies, physical activity was not a distinct aspect of life but was seamlessly woven into the fabric of daily existence. The Tarahumara people of Mexico, known for their long-distance running, and various hunter-gatherer communities, exemplify societies where exercise is not an isolated event but a natural part of life. These populations did not engage in physical activity for its own sake but as a component of necessary tasks and social interactions, such as hunting, gathering, play, and dance.

Recent research introduces the 'Active Grandparent Hypothesis,' suggesting that maintaining an active lifestyle into old age is not only possible but also beneficial for extending 'healthspan' and longevity. This supports the idea that continued physical activity plays a crucial role in slowing the aging process and improving the quality of life as we age.

Gardening as a physical activity

Gardening is an exceptional form of low-impact exercise that offers a unique combination of physical activity and nutritional benefits. It involves a variety of movements and tasks that engage the body in a gentle yet effective way. From the resistance encountered while digging and shovelling to the act of bending and stretching to plant and weed, gardening provides a low impact workout that includes strength training, flexibility, and endurance.

The resistance training aspect of gardening comes from handling heavy materials like soil and compost, which requires a significant amount of physical effort. This kind of natural resistance training not only helps build muscle strength but also improves bone density and joint health. The repetitive nature of many gardening tasks, such as digging, planting, and raking, can enhance hand strength and dexterity.

Gardening can offer huge nutritional advantages, particularly when it involves growing fruits, vegetables, salad items, and herbs. This practice transforms gardening from a hobby into a source of fresh, organic produce that can significantly impact your diet and overall health. The act of growing your own food encourages a deeper connection to what you eat, often leading to healthier eating habits and a greater intake of vital nutrients.

Gardening allows people to control what goes into their food. By avoiding synthetic pesticides and fertilisers, home gardeners can enjoy the health benefits of organic produce without the premium price often associated with organic foods. This organic produce is not only better for the environment but also for our health, offering higher levels of beneficial antioxidants and nutrients.

The act of caring for plants and being outdoors can reduce stress, improve mood, and increase feelings of joy and satisfaction. The combination of physical activity, exposure to sunlight, and the calming nature of gardening work together to enhance mental health.

Chapter Summary & Key Points

- A modern sedentary lifestyle, driven by technological advancements such as cars and desk jobs, has led to increased health issues due to our bodies being designed for movement.

- A high fibre diet, consisting of plant-based foods, is crucial for people leading sedentary lifestyles, offering benefits such as increased feelings of fullness without added calories.

- Regular physical activity enhances physical and mental health without the need for extreme forms of exercise.

- Contrary to the modern perception of aging as a decline in physical activity, maintaining physical activity into old age can improve quality of life and extend healthspan.

- Gardening serves as a form of low-impact exercise that offers both physical and nutritional benefits, such as strength training and flexibility, while also contributing to mental well-being through stress reduction and increased outdoor activity.

- Learn to cook. Eat less processed food and eat more veg. Even better try to grow it yourself if you can.

CHAPTER 4
MACRONUTRIENTS; PROTEIN

Protein stands as one of the pillars of a balanced diet, vital for the maintenance and development of muscle mass, the repair of body tissues, and the seamless execution of various body and nerve functions. Its significance extends to, influencing weight management, muscle preservation, and overall satiety (feeling full).

Sources of protein

As with all nutrients, I stand on the platform that it is best to get your protein from whole foods and not supplements and powders.

The best sources are those that contain "complete" proteins. Complete proteins are foods that contain all nine essential amino acids in enough quantities that our bodies need to maintain a good level health and functioning. Essential amino acids are those that the human body cannot make on its own and must be obtained through diet. The concept of complete proteins is particularly important in nutrition because amino acids are the building blocks of proteins, which, in turn, are necessary for various bodily functions such as building and repairing tissues, making enzymes and hormones, and supporting immune function.

Most animal-based foods like meats, eggs & dairy are considered complete proteins. Animal sources of protein are typically complete because they closely match the amino acid profile needed by the human body. These animal sources for protein can lead to an intake of higher levels of saturated fats and cholesterol, particularly in red meat where the saturated fat is marbled through the meat, compared to chicken and turkey where the saturated fat is mostly in the skin. Because of this it is best to look at both animal products and plants as sources of protein.

Some plant-based foods are considered complete proteins and are vital for vegetarians and vegans. These are plants like quinoa, buckwheat, seeds (chia seeds & hemp seeds), soybeans and soybean products like tempeh and tofu.

In Ireland, the trend of adding excessive protein to foods and supplements is significant. This practice often capitalises on the perception of all protein as inherently healthy, leading to an unnecessary increase in consumption. Many Western diets already provide more than enough protein, making additional supplementation unnecessary. This excessive intake can not only strain the kidneys but also divert attention from the importance of a varied diet that includes other essential nutrients. The reality is that very few people in developed countries are deficient in protein, thanks to the abundance and variety of protein sources available.

Muscle Mass and Repair

At the cellular level, protein is crucial for building, maintaining, and repairing muscle tissue. During exercise, muscle fibres undergo stress, leading to micro-tears in the muscles. The body uses protein to repair these tears, which, in turn, leads to stronger and larger muscles. This process determines the importance of adequate protein intake for athletes and people engaged in regular physical activity.

When you visit a gym and get an assessment you will likely be advised to increase your protein intake by the fitness instructor. This is not only because of the effect it has on muscle repair but also its ability to provide satiety which will lead you to not overconsume calories. This overconsumption of protein is going to be at the expense of fresh fruit and vegetables which provide far more nutritional bang for your buck per portion and will also help you feel fuller for longer.

Supporting Weight Management

Protein's satiating effect is well-documented, with studies showing that it can help prevent overeating by promoting feelings of fullness. This can be particularly beneficial for those trying to manage their weight or reduce snacking on high-calorie foods. Protein helps stabilise blood sugar levels, which can curb cravings and prevent the energy spikes and dips associated with high-carbohydrate diets. The role of hormones like ghrelin (the hunger hormone) and peptide YY (which makes you feel full) is crucial in this context. By influencing these hormones, protein intake can directly affect our hunger signals and satiety, making it a key player in weight management strategies.

Contrary to popular belief or what your gym instructor may say protein deficiency is rare in western diets. Most people consuming a varied diet meet or exceed their daily protein requirements. The focus should be on the quality of protein sources rather than quantity alone. Consuming too much protein at once can lead to it being converted into fat and carbohydrates in the body, underscoring the need for moderation and balance. The body can absorb only a certain amount of protein at a time, making it fruitless to consume excessive amounts in one sitting.

How much protein should you consume?

The recommended daily intake of protein varies depending on factors including age, sex, weight, health status, and level of physical activity. For adults, the recommended daily intake is regarded to be 0.8 grams of protein per kilogram of body weight per day for the average adult. Bear in mind that this recommendation is designed to cover over 90% of the population so chances are if you are sedentary for most of the day, this amount will more than have you covered.

For example, a person weighing 70 kilograms should aim to consume at least 56 grams of protein daily. Pregnant and breastfeeding women should probably consume an extra 10-20 grams of protein per day to support foetal development and milk production.

Elderly people could increase their protein intake up to 1.2 grams per kilogram of body weight per day, to help preserve muscle mass and strength and physically active people may look to this figure also for the same reasons. Very physically active people could even look towards a figure of 2.0 grams of protein per kilogram of body weight to avoid injury as their muscles would be under a greater workload.

It's worth noting that even if you do need a bit more protein than your recommended daily allowance, chances are just by consuming a western diet, these additional needs are more than covered.

It's important to distribute protein intake evenly throughout the day and to pair it with a balanced diet rich in fruits, vegetables, whole grains, and healthy fats. If there is a health condition or an extreme level of activity that you think needs additional consideration, consulting with a healthcare provider or a registered dietitian can help determine the most appropriate protein intake for your health needs and lifestyle factors.

Proteins you should have in your home and include in your diet are:

Eggs: Eggs are one of the most complete sources of protein, containing all nine essential amino acids. They are also rich in vitamins, minerals, and healthy fats. Eating eggs can help with muscle repair, support brain health due to their choline content, and keep you full for longer.

Chicken Breast: Chicken breast is a lean source of protein, low in fat, and high in essential nutrients like B vitamins and selenium. It's excellent for muscle growth and repair, and its low-fat content makes it a good option for those managing their weight.

Greek Yoghurt: Greek yoghurt is thicker and creamier than regular yoghurt and contains more protein per serving. It may also contain probiotics, which are beneficial for gut health, and is a good source of calcium, supporting bone health. Use it as a mayo replacement in dips and salads or drizzle over curries.

Lentils: Lentils are a plant-based protein source that's high in fibre, iron, and folate. They're great for maintaining heart health, aiding digestion, and stabilising blood sugar levels. They're also very versatile and can be used in soups, salads, or as a meat substitute in various dishes like bolognese or curries.

Tofu: Tofu is made from soybeans and is a complete protein, meaning it contains all the essential amino acids. It's low in calories and rich in calcium, magnesium, and iron. Tofu supports heart health and bone density and can be a great protein source for vegetarians and vegans in stir fries. Grill in a hot pan or it can be blended into dips and desserts like a tofu chocolate mousse.

Quinoa: Quinoa is a grain that's also a complete protein. It's high in fibre, magnesium, B vitamins, and antioxidants. Quinoa supports healthy digestion, helps regulate blood sugar levels, and is a good option for those with gluten intolerance. Great option as an alternative to rice or add to salads.

Almonds: Almonds are a good source of plant-based protein, healthy fats, fibre, vitamin E, and magnesium. They support heart health, promote healthy skin, and help with weight management due to their satiating effects.

Cottage Cheese: Cottage cheese is low in fat but high in protein, particularly casein, which is a slow-digesting protein. This makes it a good option for a bedtime snack to support muscle repair overnight. It's also rich in calcium, which supports bone health. Use as a creamy sauce replacement in lasagne or as a breakfast bowl topped with berries and nuts/seeds.

Tinned Tuna: Tinned tuna is a convenient and affordable source of protein, rich in omega-3 fatty acids, which are important for heart and brain health. It's also a good source of selenium and vitamin D. Choose tuna in water rather than oil to keep the fat content low. Use in salads and in pasta dishes and potato cakes.

Chickpeas: Chickpeas, also known as garbanzo beans, are a great plant-based protein source. They're high in fibre, which aids digestion, and provide essential vitamins and minerals like iron, zinc, and folate. They can be used in curries, salads, stews, or made into hummus.

Turkey Breast: Turkey breast is a lean and high-protein meat, like chicken but slightly richer in certain nutrients like selenium and zinc. It's also low in fat and provides tryptophan, an amino acid that helps produce serotonin, which is beneficial for mood regulation and sleep. A cooked turkey breast will be a great roast dinner with lots of sandwich meat leftover, just don't overcook it!

Oily Fish: Oily fish like salmon, mackerel, and sardines are excellent sources of high-quality protein and omega-3 fatty acids, which are crucial for heart and brain health. These fish are also rich in vitamin D, B vitamins, and selenium. Regular consumption of oily fish can reduce inflammation, support cognitive function, and improve hearth health. Try to eat oily fish twice a week.

Chapter Summary & Key Points

- Protein is essential for muscle mass development and repair, body tissue repair, and the proper function of body and nerve systems.

- It's recommended to get protein from whole foods rather than supplements. Complete proteins, which contain all nine essential amino acids, are found in most animal-based foods and some plant-based foods like quinoa, buckwheat, and soy products.

- In Western diets, excessive protein consumption is common and can strain the kidneys and overshadow the importance of a varied diet. The focus should be on the quality of protein sources rather than quantity.

- Protein supports muscle repair post-exercise and helps manage weight by stabilising blood sugar levels and reducing cravings through its satiating effect.

- The recommended daily protein intake varies, but chances are you are already consuming more than enough.

- Learn to cook. Eat less processed food and eat more veg rather than concentrating on protein from meat only.

CHAPTER 5
MACRONUTRIENTS; FATS

Fats have received really bad press coverage since about the 1980s, when the latest weight loss craze was minimal consumption of fat in all its forms. The truth is the right fats play a huge role in a healthy diet. Healthy fats, including monounsaturated and polyunsaturated fats, play crucial roles in our body's functions, contributing to heart health, brain function, and overall well-being.

Healthy Fats

Healthy fats, such as monounsaturated and polyunsaturated fats, are essential for numerous bodily functions. These fats help absorb vitamins A, D, E, and K, and are vital for maintaining cell health and function. Despite what you may think, healthy fats contribute to heart health by improving blood cholesterol levels, reducing the risk of heart disease.

Omega-3 fatty acids, a type of polyunsaturated fat, are particularly beneficial for heart health. They have been shown to reduce inflammation throughout the body, lower levels of bad cholesterol (LDL), and increase good cholesterol (HDL). By doing so, omega-3 fatty acids help to prevent the buildup of harmful plaques in the arteries, reducing the risk of stroke and heart attack.

These omega-3 fatty acids, play a significant role in brain health. They are integral components of the brain's structure, influencing memory, learning, and cognitive function. Adequate intake of these healthy fats has been linked to a lower risk of cognitive decline and neurodegenerative diseases, such as Alzheimer's disease.

Sources of Healthy Fats

Incorporating healthy fats into your diet might seem confusing at first, but it's easier than many people believe. One of the simplest ways to do this is by focusing on the consumption of monounsaturated and polyunsaturated fats, which are not only essential for overall health but also have specific benefits for your heart and brain.

Monounsaturated fats, for example, are abundant in olive oil, avocados, and a variety of nuts and seeds. These fats are known for their ability to promote heart health by improving cholesterol levels, reducing the risk of heart disease. Polyunsaturated fats, which include the essential omega-3 and omega-6 fatty acids, can be found in fatty fish like salmon, mackerel, and sardines, as well as from walnuts, flaxseeds, and soybean oil. These fats are rich in essential omega-3 and omega-6 fatty acids, which play a significant role in heart and brain health, supporting overall well-being. For those focusing on omega-3 fatty acids, while fatty fish stand out as a prime source, plant-based alternatives such as flaxseeds, chia seeds, and walnuts are also great options. Additionally, omega-3 supplements, available in forms like fish oil or algae oil, offer a convenient alternative for people who might struggle to meet their dietary needs through food alone. This multifaceted approach to incorporating healthy fats into your diet underscores the versatility and accessibility of these nutrients, making it easier for you to enjoy the myriad health benefits they offer.

Extra virgin olive oil deserves a particular mention for both its flavour and health benefits, it stands out for being rich in monounsaturated fats and antioxidants. Although it's true that extra virgin olive oil can degrade when exposed to heat, it remains a healthier option compared to many vegetable oils, which can contain higher levels of polyunsaturated fats and may undergo heavy processing. Extra virgin olive oil's nutrient density, including its antioxidant content, makes it a valuable addition to the diet, even if some degradation occurs during cooking. Its versatility and health benefits make it an essential staple in my kitchen.

The Importance of Minimally Processed Fats

When it comes to choosing foods in your diet, the level of processing is a critical factor to consider. Minimally processed fats, such as real butter, retain more of their natural nutrients and are free from additives found in many processed products. A comparison can be drawn with "healthy" low-fat spreads, which may contain numerous ingredients, including emulsifiers, colorants, and preservatives, making them ultra-processed. These additives can detract from the health benefits of the fats and introduce unwanted chemicals into your diet. Opting for fats with fewer ingredients ensures you're consuming the nutrient as nature intended, with minimal processing and maximum health benefits.

The debate between full fat and low-fat dairy products centres on their saturated fat and calorie content. While low fat dairy is often marketed as a healthier choice due to its lower saturated fat and calorie content, this doesn't tell the whole story. Full fat dairy products contain higher levels of fat-soluble vitamins and nutrients, which are reduced or removed in low fat versions. These nutrients, including vitamins A, D, E, and K, are crucial for health and are more readily absorbed when consumed with fat. The nutritional quality of full fat dairy is generally superior to that of low-fat dairy products. While it's important to consider individual dietary needs and health goals (such as reducing your intake of saturated fats), incorporating full fat dairy can provide valuable nutrients often missing from low fat alternatives. Just be aware of the amount of these fats you are eating and maybe eat less minimally processed dairy product (like real butter and full fat yogurt) compared to more of a heavily processes spreads and low-fat flavoured dairy products.

It's important to stress that heart disease associated with saturated fat consumption is significant in Ireland, and many people should not choose full fat dairy on advice from medical professionals. However, it is puzzling why these people are often advised to consume processed dairy spreads instead of extra virgin olive oil as a butter replacement. Extra virgin olive oil is a minimally processed fat that offers numerous health benefits, including heart health, making it a potentially better alternative to processed spreads for those needing to reduce saturated fat intake.

Fats & Weight Management

Contrary to the belief that fats contribute to weight gain, healthy fats can aid in weight management. They provide a sense of satiety (a feeling of fullness) after meals, reducing the overall intake of calories. Additionally, fats help to regulate blood sugar levels by slowing the absorption of carbohydrates, which can prevent insulin spikes and crashes, making it easier to maintain a healthy weight.

In reality, diets high in healthy fats, such as the Mediterranean diet, are rarely associated with weight gain. The Mediterranean diet, celebrated for its numerous health benefits, is rich in sources of healthy fats like olive oil, nuts, and fatty fish. This diet pattern is often cited as the optimal approach to eating, not only for heart health but also for sustainable weight management. The key lies in the type of fat consumed, not the quantity. Healthy fats provide satiety helping to reduce overall calorie intake by keeping you fuller for longer, supporting weight management.

Practical advice

Choose real butter. With only one ingredient (milk), it's far less processed than many spreads on the market. If you had a litre of double cream, you could churn your own butter in less than 40 minutes, by whipping it until the buttermilk is released from the fat and washing away the rest of the buttermilk in cold water. Just be aware it is a saturated fat and eat less of it than you would a margarine or a "healthy" spread. Irish butter is far superior to any other nations (in my opinion) and is exported all over the world. Because it rains so much in Ireland, our lush, green pastures provide an ideal environment for dairy cows. Most Irish cows are grass-fed, grazing outdoors for much of the year. This diet contributes to the higher levels of beta-carotene in the milk, which in turn gives Irish butter its distinctively rich, yellow colour and enhances its flavour profile.

For most of your cooking, extra virgin olive oil should be your only choice. Applying extra virgin olive oil directly to your meats or vegetables before cooking—rather than pouring it into the pan or roasting dish—can prevent excessive degradation from heat. This method ensures that the oil retains more of its nutritional value and flavour.

When you need an oil that can withstand higher temperatures, consider Irish cold-pressed rapeseed oil or coconut oil is great in Asian dishes (although it is a saturated fat so use it sparingly). These are fantastic for a variety of cooking methods. The higher smoke point makes them versatile for both roasting and more intense frying.

Get rid of the deep fat fryer. It's tempting to use a deep fat fryer for its convenience, especially for quickly preparing foods like chips and battered chicken. However, its more than likely the oil in your deep fryer is vegetable or sunflower oil which have a huge number of calories with little nutritional value in return and encourages the consumption of ultra-processed food foods.

Air fryers are great gadgets that offer a healthier alternative to traditional frying. They work by circulating hot air to crisp up food, more like a mini oven than a deep fat fryer, requiring minimal to no oil. While not a perfect substitute for a deep fat fryer, air fryers provide a quick and healthier option for achieving that desirable crispy texture in foods. They're an excellent tool for those looking to enjoy their favourite dishes with less oil and fat.

Fats you should have in your home and include in your diet are:

Avocados: Rich in monounsaturated fats, avocados are excellent for heart health and can be used in salads, spreads, or smoothies.

Extra Virgin Olive Oil: A staple in many kitchens, olive oil is high in monounsaturated fats and is great for cooking or drizzling over salads.

Nuts (e.g., almonds, walnuts, and cashews): These are packed with healthy fats, particularly monounsaturated and polyunsaturated fats. They make for a great snack or can be added to dishes for extra crunch.

Seeds (e.g., chia seeds, flaxseeds, and sunflower seeds): These are excellent sources of omega-3 fatty acids and other healthy fats. They can be sprinkled on cereals, salads, or blended into smoothies.

Fatty Fish (e.g., salmon, mackerel, and sardines): These are rich in omega-3 fatty acids, which are essential for heart and brain health. They are readily available in most supermarkets, either fresh, frozen, or canned. Fish is easily cooked in the oven or fish fillets like mackerel can be cooked quickly under a grill.

Coconut Oil: Contains medium-chain triglycerides (MCTs), which are a type of fat that is more easily used by the body for energy. It's versatile for cooking and baking but is a saturated fat so use sparingly as you should with coconut milk also.

Dark Chocolate: High-quality dark chocolate (70% cocoa or more) contains healthy fats and antioxidants. It can be enjoyed in moderation as a treat.

Cheese: Provides a good source of fats, including conjugated linoleic acid (CLA), which is linked to various health benefits. Cheese also offers calcium and protein.

Eggs: Particularly the yolk, eggs are a great source of healthy fats, along with essential nutrients like choline which is vital for brain health, liver function, cellular structure, metabolism, and the development of the nervous system.

Greek Yoghurt: Full-fat Greek yoghurt contains beneficial fats, probiotics, and protein, making it a nutritious addition to breakfast or snacks.

Real Irish Butter: Known for its rich flavour and creamy texture, real Irish butter is a natural source of saturated fats and fat-soluble vitamins like A, D, and E. It's perfect for spreading, cooking, and baking.

Chapter Summary & Key Points

- You need healthy fats, they are essential for absorbing vitamins, maintaining cell health, and contributing to heart and brain health by improving blood cholesterol levels and reducing the risk of diseases.

- Healthy fats can be easily incorporated into the diet through foods rich as olive oil, avocados, nuts, fatty fish, and seeds. Extra virgin olive oil is fantastic for its antioxidants and health benefits, but it does degrade when heated.

- Choose minimally processed fats like butter and full fat dairy products. Full fat dairy products contain more fat-soluble vitamins and are generally superior in nutritional quality compared to low-fat versions. Just eat less of it.

- Be careful when buying any fat source that is marketed as "healthy" these could be highly processed and contain lots of thickeners and stabilisers. Read the label and make sure you recognise all the ingredients.

- Diets high in healthy fats, such as the Mediterranean diet, support sustainable weight management and overall health.

- Learn to cook. Eat less processed food, eat more veg.

CHAPTER 6
MACRONUTRIENTS; CARBOHYDRATES

Carbohydrates are a crucial part of our diet, providing the primary source of energy for our bodies. This means that they are the fuel that your body will burn first. However, not all carbs are created equal. When you look at the volume of food you eat most, whether you follow a healthy diet or not, carbohydrates are more than likely the most consumed macro nutrients you eat. Understanding the distinction between healthy and unhealthy carbohydrates can significantly impact our overall health, influencing everything from our energy levels to our risk for chronic diseases.

Carbohydrates are one of the three macronutrients found in food, alongside proteins and fats. They are classified into three main types: sugars, starches, and fibre. The body breaks down most sugars and starches into glucose, a simple sugar that serves as a vital energy source. Fibre, on the other hand, does not provide energy directly but plays a critical role in maintaining gut health, regulating blood sugar levels, managing your hunger cravings, and feeding your good gut bacteria.

Healthy Carbs

Healthy carbohydrates stand out due to their high fibre content, vitamins, minerals, and low glycaemic index (GI). The glycaemic index is a measure of how quickly foods cause increases in blood glucose levels. Foods with a low GI value (about 55 or less) are digested, absorbed, and metabolised slower, leading to a gradual rise in blood glucose and insulin levels. This is beneficial for controlling blood sugar and maintaining energy levels.

Fruits are excellent sources of vitamins, minerals, and fibre. They also contain natural sugars, which, when consumed as part of the whole fruit, have a minimal impact on blood sugar levels due to their fibre content. The opposite happens when you blitz fruit into a smoothie or put it into a juicer; the sugar gets released from the fibre and transforms to "free sugar" which is has the same effect of your blood sugar as drinking a fizzy drink. This doesn't mean you can't enjoy an orange juice or fruit smoothie occasionally just don't be fooled into thinking it's a healthy choice.

Vegetables are packed with nutrients and fibre. Leafy greens, cruciferous vegetables like broccoli and brussels sprouts, and starchy vegetables like sweet potatoes and squash offer a wide range of healthy carbs. You can't consume too much veg so whether it's in freshly chopped in salads, stir fried, steamed, roasted, in soups, frozen (which is sometimes more nutritious than fresh vegetables) or however you like. Make sure to put your vegetables first at every meal. It's just as important to eat lots of different types of vegetables as it is to consume them in volume. Different coloured vegetables contain different antioxidant compounds that contain different health benefits. This is where the term "Eat a Rainbow" comes from. The more diverse your plant consumption the bigger the health benefits and your good gut bacteria thrive on a diet of lots of different plants.

Legumes which are essentially; beans, lentils, and peas are not only high in protein but also rich in complex carbohydrates and fibre, making them a very nutritious and a huge part of a heathy diet. Try to consume a portion of legumes every day if you can. We don't eat enough legumes in Ireland, and you should try to eat a portion every day. Baked beans and tinned peas are fine but look at the label and make sure they are not tinned with lots of added sugars and other ingredients you don't recognise. Try adding green lentils to minced beef dishes or to curries, practice making hummus from chickpeas and use tinned kidney beans and butter beans in chillis and stew. There is truth to the jokes that beans and legumes make you "windy" but this is just your gut bacteria thriving with the new foods that they are not used to, this is a very short term effect on introducing these to your diet.

Whole grains retain all parts of the grain, including the fibre-rich outer layer. Examples include quinoa, brown rice, whole wheat, oats, and barley.

Unhealthy Carbs

Refined carbohydrates are processed foods from which the natural fibre has been removed. This category includes white bread, pastries, sugary drinks, and other processed foods. Consuming refined carbs can lead to spikes in blood sugar levels, as they are quickly digested and absorbed, causing rapid increases in blood glucose and insulin levels. Over time, a diet high in refined carbs can contribute to health issues such as weight gain, obesity, type 2 diabetes, and heart disease.

These refined carbohydrates are derived from whole food sources but are processed in a way that removes the bran and germ, leaving behind the endosperm. This process significantly reduces the food's nutritional content, particularly its fibre, vitamins, and minerals. The primary goal of refining is to improve texture, extend shelf life, and enhance flavour, but this comes at a significant nutritional cost.

The lack of fibre in refined carbohydrates means that the body can digest and absorb them rapidly. This leads to quick spikes in blood glucose levels, followed by a surge in insulin release from the pancreas. Insulin is a hormone responsible for signalling cells to absorb glucose from the bloodstream for energy or storage. Frequent blood sugar spikes and the resultant insulin surges can over time lead to insulin resistance, a condition where cells become less responsive to insulin's signals. Insulin resistance is associated with a host of metabolic issues.

The rapid digestion of refined carbs can lead to overeating, as these foods are less satisfying than their whole-grain counterparts and can lead to cravings for more food shortly after consumption. This cycle of overeating can contribute to weight gain and obesity.

The concepts of glycaemic index (GI) and glycaemic load (GL) are crucial in understanding the impact of carbohydrates on blood sugar levels. Foods with a high GI are rapidly digested and absorbed, causing a swift rise in blood sugar and insulin levels. Refined carbohydrates typically have a high GI, contributing to the health risks discussed. Glycaemic load considers both the GI and the amount of carbohydrate in a serving of food, providing a more accurate representation of a food's impact on blood sugar. So, to put it into perspective a food such as a slice of white bread toasted might be high GI but if you only have a slice of it with some peanut butter (which is low GI) it won't have too big of a glycaemic load. However, if you at 2 slices of white bread toast, you might be consuming a similar number of calories, but glycaemic load will be far higher.

Carb Loading

The relationship between carbohydrate intake, glucose production, and energy utilization is particularly relevant in the context of physical activity and dietary habits for active people. For athletes and physically active people, "carb loading" is a strategy to maximise the storage of glycogen (a form of glucose stored in the liver and muscles) to enhance endurance and performance. However, for sedentary individuals, the dynamics of carbohydrate consumption and glucose metabolism can have less beneficial, and sometimes detrimental effects on health and energy levels.

During prolonged or intense physical activity, glycogen stores serve as a critical energy source. By increasing carbohydrate intake in the days leading up to the event, athletes can extend their endurance and improve performance. This process is beneficial for sportspeople because it ensures that they have a readily available source of energy that can be utilised during their activity. The body prefers glucose as a fuel source during high-intensity exercises because it can be quickly converted to energy.

Marathon runners are a prime example of this, the day before the big race they will eat a high carb evening meal the consume refined carbs before the event. During the hours long event runners will consume high sugar jellies and liquid energy gels to replace the glycogen burned during the event. This ready to use energy can slow down the dreaded "hitting the wall" which is the body's glycogen stores become depleted, so it no longer has the fuel it needs to continue running. Combined with the normal levels of fatigue at the latter stages of a race this is both physically and mentally draining. Consuming sugar and often caffeine rich gels often can prevent or delay this.

Sedentary Lifestyles & Carbs

For people with sedentary lifestyles, the dynamics of carbohydrate consumption and glucose metabolism are very different than for active people. In the absence of regular, intense physical activity, the body has limited need for immediate energy sources or extensive glycogen reserves. When carbohydrates are consumed in significant amounts by sedentary people, the body converts these carbs into glucose, leading to a rise in blood sugar levels. The pancreas responds by releasing insulin, which helps cells absorb the glucose, either to be used for immediate energy or stored as glycogen.

However, since the energy demands of sedentary people are lower, the glucose that isn't needed for immediate energy can be stored as fat. Spikes in blood sugar levels can lead to a subsequent drop in blood sugar, which often triggers cravings for sugary and starchy foods as the body seeks to quickly replenish its glucose levels. This cycle can contribute to unhealthy eating habits, weight gain, and increased risk of developing insulin resistance and type 2 diabetes over time.

For people who are sedentary (not running long distances) incorporating healthy carbohydrates into your diet is straightforward. Focus on whole, unprocessed foods and aim to include a variety of sources in your meals. Experiment with different whole grains, enjoy a colourful variety of fruits and vegetables, and incorporate legumes into your dishes for added protein and fibre.

Carbs you should have in your home and include in your diet are:

Oats: Oats can be used in porridge, smoothies, or baked into healthy cookies and granola bars. They provide sustained energy through complex carbohydrates and are rich in fibre, particularly beta-glucan, which supports heart health.

Sweet Potatoes: Roast sweet potatoes as a side dish, mash them as an alternative to regular potatoes, or use them in soups and stews. Sweet potatoes offer a lower glycaemic index for steady blood sugar levels and are packed with vitamins, minerals, and fibre.

Brown Rice: Use brown rice as a base for stir-fries, salads, or as a side dish with curries. It provides complex carbohydrates and fibre, ensuring steady energy release and supporting digestive health.

Quinoa: Incorporate quinoa into salads, use it as a base for grain bowls, or cook it as a side dish. Quinoa is a gluten-free grain that's high in protein, fibre, and essential amino acids, offering sustained energy.

Whole Wheat Bread: Use whole wheat bread for sandwiches, toast, or as a base for bruschetta. It's nutrient-dense, offering more fibre, vitamins, and minerals along with complex carbohydrates compared to white bread. Buy bread from artisan sources with minimal processing.

Legumes (Beans, Lentils, Chickpeas): Add legumes to soups, stews, salads, or use them in dips like hummus. They are rich in complex carbohydrates, protein, and fibre, providing sustained energy and satiety.

Berries (Blueberries, Strawberries, Raspberries): Enjoy berries fresh, add them to cereals and yoghurt. Berries contain fibre and have a lower glycaemic index, making them a healthy source of natural carbohydrates.

Bananas: Eat bananas as a snack, add them to smoothies, or slice them over cereals and porridge. Bananas provide quick energy with natural sugars and fibre, along with potassium for muscle function.

Butternut Squash: Roast butternut squash, blend it into soups, or add it to casseroles and salads. Butternut squash is a great source of complex carbohydrates, fibre, and various vitamins and minerals.

Carrots: Enjoy carrots raw as a snack, roast them, or add them to soups and stews. Carrots provide fibre and natural sugars that are slowly absorbed, making them a good carbohydrate source.

Broccoli: Steam, roast, or sauté broccoli, or add it to stir-fries and salads. Broccoli is high in fibre and offers complex carbohydrates along with essential vitamins and minerals.

Apples: Eat apples as a snack, slice them into salads, or bake them into desserts. Apples provide fibre and natural sugars for steady energy release, along with antioxidants and vitamins.

Oranges: Enjoy oranges fresh or add orange segments to salads. Oranges are rich in vitamin C and fibre, providing natural sugars for quick energy balanced by fibre for a slower release.

Peas: Add peas to soups, stews, or salads, or serve them as a side dish. Peas are a good source of complex carbohydrates, protein, and fibre, making them a nutritious addition to meals.

Pumpkin: Use pumpkin in soups, pies, or roast it as a side dish. Pumpkin is rich in complex carbohydrates and fibre, providing a good source of energy.

Spinach: Add spinach to salads, sauté it as a side dish, or blend it into smoothies. Spinach offers a small amount of complex carbohydrates along with fibre, vitamins, and minerals.

Tomatoes: Use tomatoes in salads, sauces, soups, or enjoy them fresh. Tomatoes provide carbohydrates in the form of natural sugars and fibre, along with a range of vitamins and antioxidants.

Lentils: Incorporate lentils into soups, stews, or salads, or use them as a base for vegetarian dishes. Lentils are rich in complex carbohydrates, fibre, and protein, offering sustained energy.

Chickpeas: Use chickpeas in salads, soups, or blend them into hummus and other dips. Chickpeas are high in complex carbohydrates, fibre, and protein, contributing to long-lasting energy and satiety.

Chapter Summary & Key Points

- Carbohydrates are essential for energy but vary in health impact, with sugars, starches, and fibre being the main types.

- Healthy carbohydrates are fruits, vegetables, legumes, and whole grains, eat as much colourful veg as you can and legumes every day. By doing this, you're not only getting the carbohydrates your body needs but loads of other nutrients along with them.

- Unhealthy carbohydrates like bread, rice and pasta has their natural fibre and nutrient removed, leading to rapid spikes in blood sugar and insulin levels. Consistent consumption can lead to weight gain, obesity, type 2 diabetes, heart disease, and metabolic syndrome.

- "Carb loading" is a strategy used by athletes to maximize glycogen stores for endurance and performance. This involves increasing carbohydrate intake before an event to enhance energy availability, beneficial for prolonged or intense physical activities.

- Unless you are likely to run a marathon or play a football match reduce your intake of refined carbs. This can lead to health issues like weight gain, insulin resistance, and type 2 diabetes.

- Learn to cook. Eat less processed food, eat more veg. Vegetables are the best form of carbohydrates.

CHAPTER 7
FIBRE

As we all look to eat healthier, focusing on fibre should be the priority for the average person. Fibre is not a macronutrient, it a form of carbohydrate, but you should consider it as an important nutrient to consume for several reasons. Firstly, it keeps you feeling fuller for longer, which is a huge advantage for anyone trying to manage their weight or avoid overeating. Foods rich in fibre typically offer a high nutritional value relative to their calorie content, providing essential vitamins, minerals, and antioxidants without adding excess calories. This nutritional density ensures that you're not only meeting your fibre needs but also getting a wide range of nutrients along with it. By promoting a feeling of satiety, a high-fibre diet helps prevent poor food decisions. When you feel full and satisfied, you're less likely to reach for unhealthy snacks or processed foods that offer little more than empty calories. This natural appetite control makes fibre the number one aspect of your diet to concentrate on for maintaining a healthy, balanced diet and making positive dietary choices.
Processing foods usually involves stripping food of fibre so by choosing foods rich in fibre chances are you are consuming your calories in a less processed form.

Soluble and Insoluble Fibre

Fibre is broadly classified into two types: soluble and insoluble, each offering unique benefits to the body.

Soluble fibre dissolves in water to form a gel-like substance, which helps to lower low-density lipoprotein (LDL) or "bad" cholesterol and reduce inflammation. These actions contribute to promoting heart health. Soluble fibre also plays a role in regulating blood sugar levels by slowing the absorption of sugar, which can help control the resulting insulin response. Soluble fibre also has anti-inflammatory properties. Chronic inflammation is linked to a host of diseases, including heart disease. By mitigating inflammation, soluble fibre contributes to a reduced risk of developing cardiovascular conditions.

Unlike its soluble counterpart, insoluble fibre does not dissolve in water. Instead, it adds bulk to the stool and helps food pass more quickly through the stomach and intestines, preventing constipation and maintaining regular bowel movements. This form of fibre is crucial for keeping the digestive system healthy. Think of it like a sweeping brush pushing all the metabolic waste trough your system.
Insoluble fibre's role in preventing constipation and promoting regular bowel movements is well-documented, while soluble fibre can benefit those suffering from diarrhoea or loose stools by absorbing water and adding bulk to the stool.

Fibre & Weight Management

Foods high in fibre tend to help you feel fuller than their low-fibre counterparts. This increased sense of fullness can significantly reduce the overall caloric intake by curbing the urge to snack on processed or high-calorie foods. The sensation of fullness, or satiety, is crucial in controlling eating habits. Fibre-rich foods absorb water and expand in the stomach, physically contributing to a feeling of fullness. Additionally, they take longer to chew and slow down the overall eating process, giving the body time to recognise when it's had enough food, which helps in reducing portion sizes and preventing overeating. Fibre rich foods tend to be harder to break down so the body requires more energy to process these foods, which can subtly boost metabolism, burning more calories without doing any extra activity.

These foods are typically less energy-dense, which means they provide fewer calories for the same volume of food compared to low-fibre options. This characteristic of fibre-rich foods makes them crucial in diets aimed at long term weight loss or and sustainable maintenance.

Fibre & Gut Health

Unlike refined carbohydrates, which get digested and absorbed in the stomach and small intestine, fibre offers a unique advantage. Fibre travels through our digestive system largely undigested until it reaches the colon, where it serves as a source of nutrients for our gut microbiota. This intricate relationship between fibre and gut health is not just beneficial but essential for our overall health.

Fibre resists stomach acid and digestive enzymes, arriving in the colon relatively intact. This undigested fibre becomes food for the beneficial bacteria residing in our gut. As these microbe's ferment fibre, they produce short-chain fatty acids (SCFAs), such as butyrate, acetate, and propionate, which are crucial for gut health. These SCFAs serve multiple roles, including nourishing colon cells, reducing inflammation, and enhancing immune function.

Fibre-rich, colourful vegetables are loaded with polyphenols. These plant-based compounds are not just antioxidants; they are also excellent fuel for gut microbes. Polyphenols can enhance microbial diversity (meaning they support lots of different types of good bacteria to thrive), fostering a gut environment that supports overall health. This synergy between fibre and polyphenols is why you should try to combine wholegrains with a wide variety of colourful vegetables, herbs and spices.

In the modern diet, all our consumption of ultra-processed foods, poses a significant threat to gut health. These foods are often low in fibre and high in refined sugars, unhealthy fats, and a huge amount of chemicals, including artificial preservatives, colourings, and flavourings. The removal of fibre in these foods deprives gut microbes of their essential nutrients, leading to a reduction in microbial diversity and abundance. This imbalance can cause a range of health issues, from inflammation to a weakened immune system and beyond. The chemicals found in ultra-processed foods further exacerbate the problem. Some of these substances can harm beneficial gut bacteria or promote the growth of harmful ones, disrupting the delicate balance of the gut microbiome. The resultant dysbiosis (microbial imbalance) is associated with various health concerns, including obesity, type 2 diabetes, heart disease, and even certain cancers.

Not too much too soon

Unlike other nutrients, there is no upper limit to fibre consumption due to far-reaching benefits for your health. By increasing your intake gradually and ensuring good hydration, you can enjoy the advantages of fibre without discomfort.
Adults should aim for at least 25 grams of fibre per day for women and 38 grams for men. Yet, the average intake in many Western countries, like Ireland, falls well below these recommendations, leading to missed health benefits and increased risk of chronic diseases.

While there is no established upper limit for fibre intake, a sudden increase can lead to digestive discomfort, such as bloating, gas, and altered bowel habits. This discomfort comes about because the gut microbiota needs time to adjust to the increased volume of fibre. To mitigate these effects, it's essential to increase fibre intake gradually over several weeks, allowing your digestive system to adapt. Remember that fibre rich foods are harder to break down so treat your digestive system as a muscle that needs to be trained before taking on too much fibre rich foods.

Drinking plenty of water, especially as you boost your fibre intake, is vital for maintaining digestive health and comfort. Fibre absorbs water as it moves through the digestive system, which helps to soften stools and promote regular bowel movements. Without sufficient water intake, the risk of constipation and discomfort increases.

Tips for Increasing Fibre Intake

- Begin by adding a few grams of fibre to your diet each week, allowing your body to adjust. For instance, introduce an extra serving of vegetables or switch to whole-grain versions of your favourite foods.
- Incorporate a wide range of fibre-rich foods into your diet. This not only prevents boredom but also ensures you get a blend of soluble and insoluble fibre, both of which are important for digestive health.
- Increase your water consumption as you up your fibre intake. Aim for at least 8 glasses of water a day, or more if you're active or it's particularly hot.
- Pay attention to how your body responds to increased fibre. If you experience discomfort, scale back a little before gradually increasing again.

Sources of Fibre

The first step towards a healthier diet begins with making informed choices about the foods we eat. Peas, beans, legumes, whole fruits, vegetables, and grains are not just superior sources of fibre; they are fundamental to a proper diet, offering benefits that supplements simply cannot match. By prioritising these whole foods, we can enjoy a diet that is not only high in fibre but also rich in essential nutrients, paving the way for optimal health and well-being.

Peas, beans, and legumes are a stellar source of fibre, but their value extends beyond being fibre rich. These foods contain proteins, vitamins, and minerals such as iron, zinc, and magnesium. Their high protein content makes them an excellent alternative for meat in vegetarian and vegan diets, providing a satiating effect that can aid in weight management.

Try recipes for spiced bean burgers, lentil-based curries (dahls) or homemade hummus from cheackpeas or any beans. Whole fruits and vegetables are not only abundant in fibre but also rich in vitamins, minerals, antioxidants, and polyphenols. These nutrients work synergistically to bolster our immune system, reduce inflammation, and protect against chronic diseases such as heart disease, diabetes, and certain cancers. Unlike processed foods or supplements, whole fruits and vegetables provide fibre in its natural form, which is more beneficial for the digestive system. The inclusion of a variety of fruits and vegetables in our diet ensures a wide range of phytonutrients, essential for optimal health.

Whole grains are another excellent source of dietary fibre. Unlike refined grains, which have been stripped of the bran and germ, whole grains retain all parts of the grain kernel, including the fibre-rich outer layer. This means they provide more nutrients, including B vitamins, iron, and other minerals. Swapping white bread, pasta, and rice for whole-grain alternatives such as whole wheat bread, brown rice, quinoa, and oats can significantly increase our fibre intake. These swaps not only enhance the nutritional profile of our meals but also contribute to a feeling of fullness, which can prevent overeating.

While fibre supplements can be beneficial in certain circumstances, they cannot replicate the complex nutritional profile of whole foods. Supplements might provide the necessary bulk to aid digestion, but they lack the vitamins, minerals, antioxidants, and phytochemicals found in natural food sources. Relying on supplements unless medically advised, misses the opportunity to improve dietary habits and enjoy the flavours and textures of whole foods.

Incorporating more fibre into our Western diet, which is often dominated by processed foods and high in saturated fats and sugars, requires conscious dietary choices. Starting the day with a whole-grain cereal or oats, opting for fruit as snacks, including a variety of vegetables in every meal, and choosing legumes or beans as a protein source a few times a week can make a significant difference. These choices not only increase fibre intake but also contribute to a more nutrient-dense diet.

High fibre foods you should have in your home and include in your diet are:

Oats: Oats can be used to make porridge, overnight oats, granola, or as an ingredient in baking (e.g., bread, or pancakes). Oats are rich in soluble fibre, particularly beta-glucan, which helps lower cholesterol levels and supports heart health. They also promote digestive health and provide sustained energy.

Chia Seeds: Chia seeds can be added to smoothies, yoghurt, oatmeal, or used to make chia pudding. They can also be sprinkled on salads or used in baking. Chia seeds are high in fibre, which aids digestion and helps regulate blood sugar levels. They also provide omega-3 fatty acids, which support heart health.

Lentils: Lentils can be used in soups, stews, salads, or as a base for veggie burgers. They can also be incorporated into curries or served as a side dish. Lentils are rich in both soluble and insoluble fibre, which helps improve digestion and supports a healthy gut. They are also a good source of plant-based protein and essential nutrients like iron and folate.

Black Beans: Black beans can be used in chilli, burritos, salads, soups, or as a side dish. They can also be mashed to make black bean burgers or dips. High in fibre and protein, black beans help regulate blood sugar levels and promote digestive health. They are also rich in antioxidants and beneficial nutrients like folate and magnesium.

Broccoli: Broccoli can be steamed, roasted, stir-fried, or added to soups, casseroles, and salads. It can also be blended into sauces or used as a topping for pizzas. Broccoli is high in fibre, which supports digestive health. It is also rich in vitamins C and K, and contains powerful antioxidants that help reduce inflammation and support immune function.

Brussels Sprouts: Brussels sprouts can be roasted, sautéed, or steamed. They can be added to salads, stir-fries, or used as a side dish.: Brussels sprouts are rich in fibre and contain compounds that support detoxification. They are also a good source of vitamins C and K, and have anti-inflammatory properties.

Quinoa: Quinoa can be used as a base for salads, added to soups, or served as a side dish. It can also be used in breakfast bowls or as a stuffing for vegetables. Quinoa is high in fibre, which aids digestion and helps maintain healthy blood sugar levels. It is also a complete protein, containing all nine essential amino acids, and is rich in minerals like magnesium and iron.

Sweet Potatoes: Sweet potatoes can be roasted, mashed, or baked. They can also be used in soups, stews, casseroles, or as a base for sweet potato fries. Sweet potatoes are high in dietary fibre, which supports digestive health. They are also rich in vitamins A and C, and have a lower glycaemic index than regular potatoes, helping to maintain stable blood sugar levels.

Apples: Apples can be eaten raw, added to salads, baked into pies, or used in smoothies. They can also be cooked into sauces or used in savoury dishes like pork with apple. Apples are high in soluble fibre, particularly pectin, which helps lower cholesterol levels and supports digestive health. They are also rich in antioxidants and vitamins, particularly vitamin C.

Carrots: Carrots can be eaten raw, roasted, steamed, or added to soups, stews, salads, and stir-fries. They can also be used in baking, such as in carrot cake. Carrots are rich in fibre, which promotes digestive health. They are also high in beta-carotene, which the body converts to vitamin A, supporting vision and immune function.

Chickpeas: Chickpeas can be used in salads, soups, stews, or curries. They are also the main ingredient in hummus and can be roasted for a crunchy snack. Chickpeas are high in both fibre and protein, making them a great food for digestive health and satiety. They also help regulate blood sugar levels and provide essential nutrients like folate and iron.

Avocados: Avocados can be added to salads, sandwiches, and wraps, or used as a base for guacamole. They can also be blended into smoothies or used as a topping for toast. Avocados are rich in fibre and healthy monounsaturated fats, which support heart health. They also provide a variety of vitamins and minerals, including potassium and folate.

Pears: Pears can be eaten raw, added to salads, baked into desserts, or poached. They can also be used in savoury dishes like roasted pork with pears.: Pears are high in soluble fibre, which helps regulate digestion and support heart health. They also provide vitamins C and K, and are rich in antioxidants.

Flaxseeds: Flaxseeds can be added to smoothies, yoghurt, oatmeal, or baked goods. They can also be sprinkled on salads or cereals. Flaxseeds are high in fibre and omega-3 fatty acids, which support heart health and reduce inflammation. They also contain lignans, which have antioxidant properties.

Whole Wheat Bread: Try to buy all your bread from an artisan baker as supermarket bread can contain preservatives, emulsifiers, and stabilisers. Whole wheat bread is high in dietary fibre, which promotes digestive health and helps maintain stable blood sugar levels. It also provides essential nutrients like B vitamins and iron.

Chapter Summary & Key Points

- Fibre is the number one nutrient we are not consuming enough of in the western world. The processing of our food removes the fibre in favour of simple carbohydrates.

- High-fibre foods provide a feeling of fullness, offer high nutritional value with fewer calories, and support good gut bacteria, contributing to overall well-being.

- Soluble fibre, which dissolves in water, helps to lower "bad" cholesterol, reduce inflammation, and regulate blood sugar levels. Insoluble fibre adds bulk to stool and supports regular bowel movements, preventing constipation.

- Fibre requires more energy to digest, potentially boosting metabolism.

- Get your fibre from foods like peas, beans, legumes, whole fruits, vegetables, and grains are recommended over supplements. Just increase your consumption of high fibre foods gradually over time as your system may not be used to it.

- Learn to cook. Eat less processed food, eat more fibre rich veg.

CHAPTER 8
THE 7/30 RULE

If you really want to eat a healthy diet, try to prioritise eating seven portions of fruit and vegetables a day over a variety of thirty different types of plants a week!

While "eat five a day" has been an effective public health message to increase fruit and vegetable consumption among populations traditionally consuming low amounts, the research always showed that consuming seven portions was more in line with optimal health.

The challenge with recommending seven portions for your daily intake is ensuring that it does not become overwhelming. Public health messages revised this down to five to be realistic in what can be achieved by the general population. The simplification of "five a day" was effective in making the message accessible and memorable, but as dietary habits evolve and public awareness about the benefits of a plant-rich diet increases, there is an opportunity to promote even more ambitious consumption goals.

It's no secret that eating more fruits and vegetables results in a healthier diet, it is an effective strategy for meeting fibre targets, particularly in Western diets where processed foods are prevalent. In our Irish diet, there is often little concern about protein deficiency as protein sources are abundant and readily consumed. This is largely due to the high consumption of processed foods where the natural fibre is often removed but these foods still contain some proteins.

You can find soluble fibre in apples and carrots, which helps to slow digestion and can improve blood sugar levels, while insoluble fibre, found in foods like green beans and whole fruits, helps food pass more quickly through the stomach and intestines. Consuming a variety of fruits and vegetables can ensure a good mix of both soluble and insoluble fibre, which are important for overall health. This variety also supports a healthy gut microbiota, which is essential for effective digestion and overall well-being.

Eating a variety of over 30 different types of plants each week is a highly effective way to ensure a rich intake of diverse nutrients, including a range of vitamins, minerals, and polyphenols. Polyphenols give plants their colour, so the more colourful you plate the more polyphenols you are taking in. This approach, often described as "eat a rainbow," is not just visually appealing but significantly beneficial to health.

Polyphenols are a group of naturally occurring compounds found abundantly in plants. They are categorised primarily into flavonoids, phenolic acids, polyphenolic amides, and other polyphenols, each abundant in different plant foods. These compounds are known for their antioxidant properties, which help in protecting the body's cells from damage caused by free radicals and oxidative stress. This action is crucial because oxidative stress is linked to multiple chronic diseases, including heart disease, diabetes, and cancers. Just burning calories leads to oxidation so these antioxidants mitigate against that.

The variety in plant consumption ensures a broader spectrum of these polyphenols, as different plants contain unique types and amounts of polyphenols. For example, onions and coffee are rich in quercetin, a flavonoid that has been shown to reduce blood pressure in hypertensive subjects. Berries, on the other hand, contain high levels of anthocyanins, known for their anti-inflammatory properties.

So, this "eat a rainbow" strategy involves consuming fruits and vegetables of various colours, each colour providing its own set of vitamins, minerals, and antioxidants. Red fruits and vegetables like tomatoes and red peppers are rich in lycopene and anthocyanins, while orange and yellow plants such as carrots and squash contain abundant beta-carotene, which the body converts into vitamin A. Green vegetables like spinach and kale are excellent sources of vitamins K, C, and E, along with a host of minerals and fibre. Blue and purple foods, like blueberries and aubergines, are not only rich in vitamins and minerals but also brimming with powerful antioxidants that may support heart health and reduce the risk of certain cancers.

Think of your body as a chemical factory, the food you take in, no matter what form, are basically a variety of chemicals, these get processed by digestion in your mouth, stomach, guts and bowel and at every stage these chemicals are transformed to different chemicals and compounds. The diversity in nutrient intake from eating a wide variety of plant foods can lead to improved gut health, as different nutrients support different types of beneficial bacteria in the gut microbiome. This variety can also help mitigate the risk of nutrient deficiencies, promoting overall health and preventing various diseases.

Front and Centre

The average person consumes around 1.5 kilograms of food per day. By prioritising fruits and vegetables, which are high in fibre and water but low in calories, a significant portion of this daily food intake becomes rich in nutrients yet moderate in calories. This is crucial for both weight management and overall health.

Fruits and vegetables are densely packed with nutrients such as vitamins, minerals, and antioxidants, and are also high in fibre. As discussed, fibre plays a key role in digestion—it not only helps to regulate digestion but also slows the absorption of sugar into the bloodstream, which can help manage blood sugar levels. More importantly, fibre has a significant impact on satiety, the feeling of fullness after eating. Foods high in fibre increase satiety more effectively than low-fibre foods, meaning they can help keep you feeling fuller for longer. This can naturally lead to a reduction in overall calorie intake.

Planning meals around fruits and vegetables—making them the centrepiece of every meal—naturally reduces room for less nutritious options. For example, starting a meal with a salad or a vegetable soup can reduce hunger, leading to less consumption of high-calorie dishes later in the meal. Similarly, snacking on fruits or vegetable sticks instead of crisps or chocolate bars can significantly reduce your intake of refined sugars and unhealthy fats, while helping you consume more of your seven a day.

This strategic approach not only ensures a high intake of essential nutrients but also reduces the likelihood of consuming junk food, which is typically high in calories, fats, and sugars but low in essential nutrients. By filling up on fruits and vegetables, you naturally crowd out unhealthy options, simply because your stomach has limited space and your body's nutritional needs are being satisfied more efficiently. Regular consumption of nutrient-dense foods can lead to changes in taste preferences and cravings. Over time, as the body adapts to a healthier diet rich in fruits and vegetables, cravings for high-sugar and high-fat foods often diminish, making it easier to stick to a healthy eating plan and avoid junk food not just out of necessity but due to a genuine preference for healthier options.

Making it work

Incorporating seven portions of fruit and vegetables into your daily diet can be easily achieved with thoughtful planning and mindful eating. Starting the day right and making smart food choices can set a positive tone for nourishing choices throughout the day.

Beginning the day with a glass of water hydrates your body after a night's sleep and kick-starts your metabolism. Adding a piece of fruit provides a quick, nutrient-rich start. Fruits are packed with vitamins, fibre, and antioxidants, offering an immediate nutrient boost. This simple act not only fuels the body with healthy energy but also sets a psychological precedent for making healthy food choices throughout the day.

For breakfast, a combination of yogurt with berries, nuts, or seeds is an excellent choice. This meal is rich in proteins, healthy fats, and fibres, which contribute to a feeling of fullness and can help prevent snacking on less healthy options later. Incorporating milk kefir adds a probiotic boost, supporting digestive health and contributing to a balanced gut microbiome.

At lunch, opting for a salad box over a traditional sandwich can significantly increase your vegetable intake. By omitting bread, there is more room for a variety of colourful vegetables. A salad box packed with greens, cherry tomatoes, cucumbers, peppers, and a protein source like chicken, tofu, or legumes, dressed with a vinaigrette or a splash of lemon juice and olive oil, can be both satisfying and nutrient dense.

For snacks, fresh fruit or vegetable sticks with hummus are perfect for maintaining energy levels between meals. The combination of carbs, protein, and fats in such snacks ensures sustained energy release without the highs and lows that come from more processed snacks. These are not only filling but also provide a good mix of nutrients.

Dinner should continue the theme of being centred around vegetables. Whether it's a vegetable stir-fry, an Italian-inspired dish like a vegetable-laden pasta primavera or ratatouille, or a dinner plate featuring a variety of steamed or grilled vegetables alongside a smaller portion of grilled meat or fish, the focus should always be on filling at least half your plate with vegetables. This not only ensures you meet your daily vegetable intake but also aligns with a balanced diet that supports overall health.

These choices contribute to a well-rounded diet that emphasizes the intake of natural, whole foods and minimizes processed items, aligning with nutritional recommendations for a healthy, balanced diet. This approach not only benefits physical health but also supports cognitive function and emotional well-being, creating a virtuous cycle of healthy eating habits.

Make your food exciting!

When you start to look at your diet in a plant first point of view, as described, it naturally leads to a more exciting culinary look at how you eat. This excitement largely stems from the need to incorporate a variety of flavours and textures to maintain interest and enjoyment in meals, promoting the use of an lots of spices and herbs. These additions not only enhance the taste of the food but also confer additional health benefits.

Spices and herbs are potent sources of antioxidants, anti-inflammatory agents, and other phytochemicals, making them powerful allies in promoting health while enhancing the flavour profile of any dish. For example, turmeric contains curcumin, known for its anti-inflammatory and antioxidant properties, while cinnamon can help regulate blood sugar levels. All of these herbs and spices count towards your intake of 30 different plants a week.

Consider the base of a typical curry. This dish starts with frying some onion in a blend of spices like cumin, coriander, turmeric, ginger, and garam masala. Each spice brings not only distinct flavours but also unique health benefits. These spices are often sautéed with ginger and garlic, which are themselves rich in antioxidants and have anti-inflammatory properties. Adding coconut milk creates a creamy, rich texture and adds its own health benefits, such as providing medium-chain triglycerides, which are known to support metabolism and heart health.

Even before adding the main vegetables or proteins, the curry sauce itself contains about 14 plant-based ingredients. This base is a mix of nutrients and phytochemicals, all contributing to the dish's health benefits and complex flavour profile. Then the vegetables are added to the curry, the dish becomes even more vibrant and nutrient dense. Vegetables like bell peppers, carrots, broccoli, and spinach contribute vitamins, minerals, and fibres, enhancing the meal's nutritional profile significantly. The diversity of vegetables not only makes the meal colourful and visually appealing but also ensures a huge amount of nutrients are consumed and a significant proportion of your 30 different types of vegetables per week.

This approach to eating encourages exploring different cuisines and recipes, making meals more of a new look at your meals than a chore. The constant variation prevents dietary boredom and can reignite a passion for cooking and eating healthily. When you explore various global cuisines, from Indian curries to Mediterranean salads to Southeast Asian stir-fries, the diet naturally becomes richer in both nutrients and flavours. This is precisely why I, as a chef, can endorse the contemporary understanding of healthy eating. If I had been presenting a nutrition seminar 30 years ago, I might have been advocating for restrictive, low-fat diets, focusing on ingredients that were steamed or poached, often resulting in meals lacking in flavour. However, today's approach is a food-positive perspective that incorporates a diverse variety of plants in our dishes, we not only add vibrant colours and textures but also enhance the flavours. This allows chefs and nutritionists like me to advocate for healthy eating in a way that is not only beneficial but also a very exciting way to eat.

Chapter Summary & Key Points

- Aim to eat seven portions of fruit and vegetables daily and incorporate thirty different types over a week.

- Planning your meals like this daily ensures a higher intake of dietary fibre, which is crucial for digestive health and can help prevent chronic diseases.

- Consuming a wide variety of plants ensures an intake of a broad spectrum of nutrients, including essential vitamins, minerals, and polyphenols, which provide significant antioxidant properties.

- By prioritising fruits and vegetables, which are high in fibre and low in calories, meals are more filling, reducing the likelihood of consuming less nutritious foods and helping with weight management.

- A plant-first approach encourages the use of a variety of spices and herbs, enhancing flavours and making meals more exciting while adding health benefits.

- Learn to cook. Eat less processed food, eat more veg.

CHAPTER 9

THE MEDITERRANEAN DIET

The Mediterranean diet is very much associated with longevity and health. This dietary pattern, primarily observed in countries like Greece, Italy, and Spain, involves a high intake of vegetables, fruits, legumes, nuts, beans, cereals, grains, fish, and unsaturated fats such as extra virgin olive oil. It includes a low consumption of meat and dairy products. The diet is not only a nutritional beneficial but also a reflection of a lifestyle that incorporates physical activity, sharing meals with others, and enjoying life.

Origins of the Mediterranean diet

The origins of the Mediterranean diet can be traced back to the ancient civilizations of the region. The Greeks and Romans, for example, had diets rich in cereals, vegetables, fruits, and olive oil, which are still staples of the Mediterranean diet today. The concept of the Mediterranean diet as we understand it today, however, was not formally recognised until the mid-20th century. Ancel Keys, an American physiologist, observed the low incidence of heart disease in Mediterranean countries compared to the United States and northern Europe. This observation led to a seven-country study that established the health benefits of the Mediterranean diet.

The climate and geography of the Mediterranean region have played a significant role in shaping its dietary patterns. The warm, sunny climate is ideal for growing a variety of fruits and vegetables, which are central to the diet. Olive trees thrive in this climate, making olive oil a dietary staple. The geography, with its vast coastlines, also promotes a high consumption of fish and seafood, providing a healthy source of omega-3 fatty acids.

Traditional agricultural practices in the region support a diverse range of crops. The diet emphasises eating foods that are in season, ensuring that meals are both fresh and nutritionally optimal. This practice not only supports local farmers but also minimises the environmental impact associated with food transportation.

Health Benefits

Most nutritional and health care professionals would recommend the Mediterranean diet as the optimal diet for maximum health benefits to the average person. In Ireland, most medical professionals endorse the Mediterranean diet as the one to follow, and I do too. Numerous food authors like Paula Mee, Dan Buettner, and Dr. Michael Greger have highlighted the health benefits of the diet, including a lower risk of heart disease, stroke, type 2 diabetes, and certain types of cancer. It is also associated with a lower risk of Alzheimer's disease and Parkinson's disease, possibly due to physical activity throughout latter stages of life. The diet's emphasis on plant-based foods, healthy fats, and lean proteins contributes to these health outcomes. The high consumption of good fats, vegetables, whole grains, and the slow consumption of meals, often in a group setting, is in fact the essence of this book. Additionally, the Mediterranean lifestyle, which includes physical activity and social engagement, complements the diet's nutritional benefits.

Fermented Foods in the Mediterranean Diet

The inclusion of fermented foods like yogurt and cheese enriches the Mediterranean diet with their unique flavours and textures but also offer substantial benefits for gut health and microbiome diversity. The emphasis on fermented dairy products, presents a viable dietary pattern for enhancing digestive health and promoting a robust and diverse gut microbiome.

Fermented foods undergo a process where natural bacteria feed on the sugar and starch in the food, creating lactic acid. This process not only preserves the foods but also creates beneficial enzymes, b-vitamins, Omega-3 fatty acids, and various strains of probiotics. In the Mediterranean diet, yogurt and cheese are prominent fermented foods that offer a unique blend of taste and nutritional benefits.

A significant portion of the immune system (up to 70%) is located in the gut. By promoting a healthy and diverse microbiome, fermented foods in the Mediterranean diet can enhance immune function, reducing the risk of infections and some chronic diseases. This may account for why people who follow a diet like the Mediterranean diet live longer on average.

"Blue Zones"

The concept of Blue Zones was popularised by Dan Buettner, who identified five regions in the world where people live exceptionally long and healthy lives. This concept is popularized in a recent Netflix documentary but originally the exploration into these areas and their link to longevity started decades ago. These areas include Ikaria in Greece, Sardinia in Italy, Okinawa in Japan, Nicoya in Costa Rica, and Loma Linda in California, USA. The common denominators among these diverse regions are not only genetic or environmental factors but significantly, lifestyle choices, particularly in diet.

While not all Blue Zones adhere strictly to a Mediterranean diet, they share similar dietary principles that contribute to their inhabitants' longevity. Each Blue Zone incorporates a diet rich in plant-based foods, demonstrating a high intake of fibre and polyphenols. The consumption of fermented foods, which promote a healthy gut microbiome, is also a common practice.

Ikaria, Greece, and Sardinia, Italy are parts of the Mediterranean region, these areas naturally follow the Mediterranean diet. Their diets are replete with local fruits, vegetables, whole grains, and olive oil. The consumption of local cheese and wine in moderation introduces beneficial fermented products and polyphenols, aligning closely with the Mediterranean diet's principles.

Okinawa, Japan's diet shares similar traits, such as a high intake of vegetables and soy-based foods, offering a rich source of fibre and polyphenols. The traditional Okinawan diet includes fermented soy products like miso and tofu, contributing to gut health and longevity.

Nicoya, Costa Rica's diet leverages locally grown fruits, vegetables, and whole grains, ensuring a fibre-rich diet. Corn and beans are staples of their cuisine, these provide not only fibre but also plant-based protein. Fermented foods, although not as prominent, are still part of their dietary practices through the consumption of fermented dairy.

Loma Linda, California is unique due to its high concentration of Seventh-day Adventists, who prefer a vegetarian diet. Their diet is rich in whole grains, nuts, and legumes, providing plenty of fibre and polyphenols.

Wine

Anyone who has visited a Mediterranean country will be aware of their love of wine. The diet encourages consuming wine with meals, approximately one glass per day for women and up to two glasses per day for men. This practice is not a dietary guideline but a reflection of the cultural traditions of Mediterranean societies, where wine is considered an integral part of the dining experience.

Numerous studies have linked moderate wine consumption with a variety of health benefits, which complement the advantages of the Mediterranean diet as a whole.

Research indicates that moderate wine consumption can improve heart health. The antioxidants found in wine, such as resveratrol, have been shown to reduce bad cholesterol levels and prevent blood clots, thereby reducing the risk of heart disease. Red wine, in particular, is rich in polyphenols, which act as antioxidants. These compounds help combat oxidative stress in the body, which is linked to various chronic diseases.

In Mediterranean cultures, wine is a vital component of social and family gatherings. The moderate consumption of wine, alongside a diet rich in plant-based foods, reflects a lifestyle that prioritises communal meals and the enjoyment of food in its natural state. This cultural practice supports mental and social well-being by reinforcing social bonds.

While the benefits of moderate wine consumption are supported by research, it is crucial to define what "moderate" means. Excessive alcohol consumption will lead to negative health outcomes, including an increased risk of chronic diseases and alcohol dependency. Also, alcohol consumption will have negative effects on the gut microbiome as alcohol will kill bacteria as we learned from sanitizing practices during Covid-19.

Modi-Med Diet

When we stand back at look at the Mediterranean diet and the diet of Blue Zones we can identify pillars; a high intake of vegetables, fruits, whole grains, and legumes; a moderate consumption of fish, poultry, and dairy; a low intake of red meat and processed foods; and the preferential use of extra virgin olive oil as the primary fat source. These components contribute to a diet rich in fibre, healthy fats, and antioxidants.

Cultural adaptation of the Mediterranean diet, or the" Modi Med diet", involves substituting traditional Mediterranean ingredients with local equivalents that share similar nutritional profiles. This approach maintains the diet's health benefits while making it more accessible and sustainable across different regions.

If we were to apply to look at our own Irish culinary landscape, with its rich agricultural heritage and access to the sea, we have plenty of ingredients that can support a Modi Med lifestyle.

While traditional Mediterranean dishes often include grains like quinoa and legumes such as lentils, Ireland's equivalents include barley, oats, and peas. Ireland's cold waters are home to a variety of oily fish such as salmon, mackerel, and herring. These fish are rich in omega-3 fatty acids, crucial for heart health and cognitive function. Incorporating these into the diet in place of the Mediterranean's sardines or anchovies can provide similar cardiovascular benefits. The tradition of fermented dairy products, such as kefir and yogurt, is deeply rooted in Irish culinary practices. These products offer a rich source of probiotics, enhancing gut health and immunity. They serve as excellent substitutes for the Greek or Turkish yogurts. Chefs in Ireland should look at applying the Mediterranean diet principals to Ireland's native ingredients to both increase the health benefits and reduce food miles. Ireland's climate supports the cultivation of robust fruits and vegetables. Root vegetables like potatoes, carrots, and beets; leafy greens such as kale and cabbage; and fruits like apples and berries can be easily integrated into the Modi Med diet. Especially when we try heritage varieties of these vegetables or grow them ourselves. These ingredients are rich in vitamins, minerals, and dietary fibre, promoting digestive health and reducing disease risk.

Chapter Summary & Key Points

- The Mediterranean diet is the optimum diet for the average person due to it being comprised of a high intake of vegetables, fruits, legumes, nuts, wholegrains, fish, and unsaturated fats, particularly olive oil, and low consumption of meat and dairy.

- The climate and geography of the region, conducive to growing a variety of fruits and vegetables and supporting a high fish consumption, play a significant role in the diet's formation.

- The inclusion of fermented foods like yogurt and cheese in the Mediterranean diet contributes to gut health and a diverse microbiome.

- The concept of Blue Zones highlights regions where people live exceptionally long and healthy lives, with diets like the Mediterranean diet.

- "Modi-Med Diet" adapts the Mediterranean diet's principles to local contexts.

- Learn to cook. Eat less processed food, eat more veg. Like they do in the mediterranean.

CHAPTER 10
MOOD FOOD

The link between food and mental wellbeing is strong, with numerous studies showing how diet affects mood and cognitive function. Certain nutrients and eating patterns play a crucial role in mental health. Diets rich in fruits, vegetables, whole grains, lean proteins, and healthy fats are linked to better mental health. These foods provide essential vitamins, minerals, antioxidants, and omega-3 fatty acids, all vital for brain function and the production of neurotransmitters.

Food for your hormones

When thinking of foods to enhance your mood, yod need to know how your food affects your hormones. Serotonin (the hormone that helps you feel good) and melatonin (the hormone that helps you sleep) are hormones that play significant roles in regulating mood, sleep, and overall well-being. Understanding the foods that can enhance their levels can help achieve a diet that promotes both mental and physical health. Serotonin is a neurotransmitter that contributes to feelings of well-being and happiness. It also plays a crucial role in regulating mood, appetite, digestion, sleep, and memory. Low levels of serotonin are often linked with depression and anxiety. To boost serotonin levels, try to consume foods rich in tryptophan, an essential amino acid that the body uses to produce serotonin.

Turkey is widely known for its high tryptophan content, which helps boost serotonin production. Eggs, particularly the yolks, are another excellent source of this nutrient. Aged cheeses are rich in this amino acid as well. Salmon offers not only tryptophan but also omega-3 fatty acids, which support brain health. Nuts and seeds, like pumpkin seeds, sunflower seeds, and walnuts, are great for increasing tryptophan intake. Soy products such as tofu, tempeh, and soy milk also contain high levels of tryptophan. Pineapples have bromelain, an enzyme that enhances the body's use of tryptophan. Spinach and other leafy greens provide magnesium, aiding the conversion of tryptophan to serotonin. Whole grains, such as oats, are good sources of tryptophan and help maintain steady serotonin levels. Incorporating these foods into your diet can significantly improve mood by increasing serotonin production. A higher level of serotonin enhances feelings of happiness and well-being, reduces anxiety, and promotes better sleep. It also helps regulate appetite and digestion, contributing to overall mental and physical health.

Melatonin is a hormone that regulates the sleep-wake cycle, signalling the body when it is time to sleep and wake up. Its production is influenced by light exposure; darkness promotes melatonin production, while light suppresses it. Low levels of melatonin can lead to sleep disorders and disturbances. To enhance melatonin production, consider including certain foods in your diet. Cherries, especially tart cherries, are one of the few natural sources of melatonin. Red grapes also contain melatonin, though the amount varies based on the type of grape and its ripeness. Tomatoes help support the sleep-wake cycle as they contain melatonin as well. Drinking milk before bed can boost melatonin levels, promoting better sleep. Fatty fish like salmon, mackerel, and sardines are rich in vitamin B6, which helps convert tryptophan into melatonin. Nuts, such as almonds and walnuts, contain melatonin and magnesium, which promote sleep. Goji berries are known for their high levels of melatonin. Whole grains like oats can also help increase melatonin production.

Additionally, kiwis are an excellent food choice for supporting a good night's sleep. They are rich in antioxidants and serotonin, which can help improve sleep quality and duration. Including kiwis in your diet can contribute to better sleep by enhancing your body's natural melatonin production.

Brain food

Omega-3 fatty acids, found in fatty fish like salmon, mackerel, and sardines, as well as in flaxseeds and walnuts, are essential for brain health. They help maintain the structure and function of brain cells and are linked to lower rates of depression and anxiety. These fats keep cell membranes flexible and support communication between brain cells, crucial for good cognitive function and mood regulation. B vitamins, especially folate and vitamin B12, are important for energy and making neurotransmitters like serotonin and dopamine, which control mood. Getting enough of these vitamins helps prevent depression and fatigue. Folate is in leafy greens, legumes, and fortified foods, while vitamin B12 is found in meat, dairy, and eggs. Low levels of these vitamins can cause mood disorders and low energy.

Magnesium, found in leafy greens, nuts, and seeds, has a calming effect on the nervous system. It helps regulate neurotransmitters and can reduce anxiety, supporting overall mental wellbeing.

Foods high in polyphenols, which are powerful antioxidants, also contribute to brain health. Berries, dark chocolate, and green tea are rich sources of polyphenols that protect the brain from oxidative stress and inflammation. These antioxidants help neutralise free radicals, thereby preventing damage to brain cells and supporting cognitive function. By reducing oxidative stress and inflammation, polyphenols can help mitigate the risk of cognitive decline and mood disorders, promoting overall brain health and mental clarity.

Hydration

Adequate hydration is essential for optimal brain function. Water is a vital component of the brain, influencing various cognitive processes. Dehydration can significantly impair cognitive abilities, leading to poor concentration, fatigue, and mood disturbances. When the body is dehydrated, the brain's efficiency declines, affecting memory, attention span, and overall mental clarity. This can result in difficulty focusing, increased irritability, and a sense of mental fatigue. Drinking enough water throughout the day supports cognitive performance by ensuring that brain cells remain well-hydrated and function efficiently. Proper hydration helps maintain the balance of fluids and electrolytes in the body, which is crucial for the transmission of electrical signals between neurons. This supports quicker information processing and better decision-making abilities.

Good hydration is linked to emotional stability. Dehydration can lead to alterations in mood, causing feelings of anxiety, irritability, and even mild depression. By maintaining proper hydration levels, you can experience a more balanced mood.

Sugar

Diets high in processed and sugary foods are strongly linked to increased inflammation and a higher risk of depression. These foods often cause rapid changes in blood sugar and insulin levels, which lead to mood swings and energy crashes. Consuming high amounts of sugar and refined carbohydrates can create a cycle of spiking and crashing blood sugar levels, which can negatively impact mood and overall mental wellbeing. Reducing the intake of these foods helps maintain a more stable mood by preventing these rapid fluctuations.

On the flip side, complex carbohydrates found in whole grains, legumes, and vegetables provide a steady source of energy. Unlike simple sugars, complex carbohydrates release glucose slowly into the bloodstream, which helps to stabilise blood sugar levels and prevent mood swings. This steady release of energy supports consistent mental and physical performance throughout the day.

Eating regular, balanced meals that include a variety of nutrients is crucial for keeping blood sugar levels stable, thereby supporting mood regulation. Skipping meals or eating irregularly can lead to hypoglycaemia, a condition characterised by low blood sugar levels. Hypoglycaemia (abnormally low levels of blood sugar) can cause you symptoms such as irritability, anxiety, and fatigue, which can significantly affect mental wellbeing. So, maintaining a regular eating schedule with balanced, nutrient-rich meals is essential for sustaining a stable mood and optimal mental health.

Gut health and the brain

The gut-brain axis is a two-way communication system between your digestive system and your brain, meaning the foods you eat can significantly influence your mental wellbeing, and your mental state can also affect your gut health. Consuming nutrient-rich, gut-friendly foods sets you up for better overall health and a more positive mood. However, eating ultra-processed foods can disrupt your gut microbes, negatively affecting brain function and mood. If you consistently consume poor-quality food, you cannot expect to achieve a good quality mood. A healthy gut microbiome is supported by a diet rich in probiotics, beneficial bacteria found in fermented foods such as yoghurt, kefir, sauerkraut, and kimchi. These probiotics help maintain the balance of good bacteria in the gut, essential for optimal digestive health and, consequently, mental wellbeing. Research shows that an imbalance in gut bacteria (dysbiosis) can negatively impact mental health. Dysbiosis is associated with increased inflammation and a compromised ability to produce neurotransmitters, chemicals that transmit signals in the brain. This imbalance has been linked to various mental health issues, including depression and anxiety.

The gut microbiome significantly influences serotonin production, with around 90% of the body's serotonin produced in the gut. This highlights the critical role that gut health plays in emotional regulation. A diverse and balanced gut microbiome supports serotonin and other important neurotransmitters, enhancing mood and cognitive function. However, good mental health requires a holistic approach. While a nutritious diet is crucial, it's not the only factor. Managing your external environment is also essential, involving reducing exposure to anxiety and stress and engaging in activities that promote relaxation and mindfulness. Practices such as meditation, yoga, and regular physical exercise can help manage stress levels and improve mental resilience.

By combining a healthy diet with mindful environmental and lifestyle choices, you can better support both your gut health and mental wellbeing, setting yourself up with a better chance to feel great and thrive in all aspects of life.

Chapter Summary & Key Points

- Food and mental wellbeing are deeply interconnected. Diets rich in fruits, vegetables, whole grains, lean proteins, and healthy fats promote better mental health outcomes due to essential nutrients.

- Serotonin and melatonin, crucial for mood and sleep regulation, can be boosted through diet.

- Foods like fatty fish, flaxseeds, walnuts, leafy greens, legumes, berries, dark chocolate, and green tea are beneficial.

- Good hydration is essential for optimal brain function, cognitive performance, and emotional stability. Dehydration can impair memory, concentration, and mood. Drink more water.

- The gut-brain axis, influenced by gut microbiome health, plays a significant role in mental health, with probiotics in fermented foods promoting a healthy gut and better mood regulation.

- Learn to cook. Eat less processed food, eat more veg. It's great for your mood.

CHAPTER 11
HYDRATION AND DRINKS

Hydration refers to maintaining an appropriate level of water in the body, which is indispensable for regulating body temperature through sweating and facilitating cellular functions and chemical reactions, including metabolism. Water transports nutrients and oxygen to cells, removes waste products, cleanses the body, and lubricates and cushions joints, protecting tissues and organs from shock and damage.

Hydration and nutrition are deeply interconnected. Adequate hydration is essential for proper digestion and nutrient absorption, as water is a component of saliva and gastric juices that break down food and dissolve nutrients for absorption into the bloodstream. Water is also necessary for metabolic processes that convert food into energy. When dehydrated, these processes become less efficient, making it difficult for the body to metabolise stored fat or carbohydrates.

Nutrients dissolved in bodily fluids are transported to different parts of the body. Adequate hydration ensures these fluids are sufficiently diluted and flowing freely to deliver nutrients where they are needed.

Dehydration

Dehydration occurs when you use or lose more fluid than you take in, and your body doesn't have enough water and other fluids to carry out its normal functions. If left unchecked, dehydration can lead to serious complications.

Dehydration manifests through a variety of symptoms and has significant effects on the body. Initially, you may experience thirst, which is an early sign that your body is already low on fluids. This is often accompanied by a reduction in urine output, which becomes noticeably darker, deviating from its normal light yellow or clear colour. Early indicators also include a dry mouth and lips, alongside fatigue or dizziness, due to the impact of fluid loss on blood volume. Commonly, dehydration leads to headaches as a result of decreased blood flow and oxygen to the brain, and in more severe cases, it can inhibit tear production and cause eyes to appear sunken, a symptom particularly prominent in children. Another telltale sign is a loss of skin elasticity, where skin that is pinched does not bounce back quickly.

Beyond these symptoms, dehydration can severely disrupt bodily functions. It can diminish cognitive abilities, making it harder to think clearly or perform tasks effectively. The digestive system also suffers, as adequate water is essential for preventing constipation and other digestive problems. Long-term, insufficient hydration can lead to the formation of kidney stones and even cause kidney damage. Furthermore, dehydration disrupts the balance of critical electrolytes such as sodium and potassium, which are vital for numerous physiological processes. In extreme cases, it can lead to hypovolemic shock, where diminished blood volume results in a dangerous drop in blood pressure and reduced oxygen levels, posing immediate health risks.

Alcohol

Historically, the consumption of fermented beverages predates recorded history. There is evidence suggesting that early humans intentionally fermented fruits and grains to produce alcoholic drinks. In ancient times, clean and safe drinking water was not always readily available. Fermented beverages such as beer and wine underwent a boiling process during production, killing harmful pathogens found in water sources. Thus, drinking these beverages was often safer than consuming water directly from rivers or streams, which could be contaminated with bacteria or parasites.

As civilizations evolved, so too did the production and consumption of alcohol. It became an integral part of religious rituals, medicinal practices, and daily life in many societies. In medieval Europe, for instance, beer and wine were common daily drinks among all ages and classes. The development of brewing and vinification skills was considered advanced technology for its time and contributed to economic and social structures within growing cities.

In many cultures, sharing a drink is a sign of trust and friendship. It can play a part in business negotiations, celebrations, and rituals. This aspect of alcohol as a facilitator of social interaction has been pivotal in its enduring presence in human culture. Alcohol has the unique ability to bring people together, fostering a sense of community and belonging. Social drinking settings, from ancient communal feasts to modern bars and gatherings, facilitate bonding and help to weave the social fabric of societies.

Alcohol can lower inhibitions, making people more open to conversation and shared experiences, which can strengthen social ties and promote cohesion within groups. For this reason, I enjoy a drink. If I'm honest, I have probably been known to have a few drinks too many on occasion. While socialising with alcohol is not beneficial to health, it does reinforce a sense of community with those you spend your time with.

As mentioned previously, red wine is particularly rich in a type of polyphenol called resveratrol, which has been studied for its potential cardiovascular benefits. Polyphenols are naturally occurring, beneficial compounds found in plants, including the grapes used to make wine. These compounds are thought to act as antioxidants, reducing oxidative stress in the body which is linked to a variety of chronic diseases. Resveratrol is believed to help reduce inflammation and lower the risk of heart disease and certain cancers. However, the amount of resveratrol in red wine is quite small, and the health benefits of moderate red wine consumption may also be influenced by other factors such as the dietary and lifestyle patterns commonly seen in populations that consume wine regularly.

Despite the potential benefits of polyphenols, it's essential to remember that alcohol itself is a toxin that can have various adverse effects on health. Ethanol, the type of alcohol found in alcoholic beverages, is metabolised by the liver into acetaldehyde, a toxic chemical, and a probable carcinogen. Regular consumption of alcohol can lead to an array of health issues, including liver diseases such as fatty liver, fibrosis, and cirrhosis, as well as other conditions like pancreatitis.

Alcohol consumption can also affect brain function, causing changes in behaviour, mood, and cognitive processes. Chronic alcohol use is detrimental to the brain, leading to a risk of long-term cognitive decline and memory issues. Furthermore, alcohol is calorically dense yet nutritionally poor, contributing to weight gain and interfering with nutrient absorption, which can result in nutritional deficiencies.

Alcohol consumption can also significantly impact the gut microbiome, the vast community of microorganisms residing in the digestive system that play a crucial role in health and disease. Alcohol affects the balance and composition of these microbial communities, which can influence everything from digestion to immune function. Research indicates that even moderate alcohol consumption can disrupt the gut barrier, leading to increased gut permeability (sometimes referred to as "leaky gut") and allowing more harmful substances to pass into the bloodstream.

This disruption can lead to an imbalance in the gut flora (dysbiosis), which has been associated with a wide range of health issues, including inflammatory bowel disease, obesity, and even mental health disorders. The changes in the microbiome may also reduce the production of short-chain fatty acids, which are vital for colon health and immune function.

Soft Drinks

Soft drinks are a common form of refreshment in many western countries, but they come with significant nutritional drawbacks, particularly due to their high sugar content. The term "empty calories" is very much apt to describe the calories derived from most soft drinks; these provide substantial energy but minimal nutritional benefit. This is particularly concerning considering that a single can of a typical soft drink can contain upwards of nine teaspoons of sugar, far exceeding the daily limit recommended by health organisations. The sugar in soft drinks contributes to a range of health issues. Not only does it increase the risk of obesity, but it's also linked to type 2 diabetes, cardiovascular disease, and tooth decay. The body breaks down these sugars rapidly, causing a spike in blood sugar and insulin levels, which can lead to insulin resistance over time.

In response to the health concerns associated with sugar, many manufacturers offer zero-sugar versions of their products. These beverages are sweetened with artificial sweeteners like aspartame, sucralose, or saccharin. While these provide a sweet taste without the added calories, they're not free from health concerns. Some research suggests that these chemical sweeteners can negatively affect the gut microbiome, the complex community of micro-organisms in our digestive systems. This disruption can impact everything from digestion to immune function. While these sweeteners are considered safe by regulatory bodies, there is ongoing debate about their long-term health effects, especially when consumed in large amounts. One significant concern is the potential impact of artificial sweeteners on appetite regulation. The theory suggests that when you consume an artificially sweetened drink, your body anticipates a sugar intake and prepares an insulin response. However, because no actual sugar enters the bloodstream, the body continues to crave carbohydrate energy. This craving may lead to an increased desire for sugary and starchy foods, potentially undermining efforts to reduce calorie intake and manage weight.

Energy drinks pose another concern, especially for younger people. These beverages not only contain high levels of sugar but also significant amounts of caffeine and other stimulants, such as taurine and guarana. These compounds can lead to serious health issues in youths, including heart palpitations, high blood pressure, and in extreme cases, cardiac arrest. The high caffeine content can also affect the developing brains of children and teenagers, potentially leading to anxiety, sleep disturbances, and disrupted attention spans.

If you are someone that consumes a lot of soft drinks, water emerges as the best choice for hydration. It provides the hydration your body needs without any added sugars, calories, or artificial ingredients. For those who prefer a bit of variety, carbonated water is a good alternative. It offers the same benefits as still water, with the added appeal of fizziness, without the health risks associated with soft drinks.

Fruit Juices and Smoothies

Fruit juices are often perceived as a healthy choice; however, they present several nutritional drawbacks compared to whole fruits. The primary issue with fruit juice is that it involves extracting the liquid from fruits while leaving behind the pulp, which contains the fibre. Fibre is crucial not only for digestive health but also for slowing the absorption of sugar into the bloodstream. Without this fibre, the natural sugars in fruit juice are absorbed more rapidly, leading to quicker spikes in blood sugar levels. This rapid absorption can be particularly concerning for people with insulin resistance or diabetes.

Frequent consumption of fruit juices can contribute to excessive calorie intake. Many people do not realise how many fruits are required to produce a single glass of juice, which can lead to unintentional overconsumption of sugars.

Smoothies might seem like a healthier option since they often include the whole fruit, retaining the fibre that is lost in juicing. However, the process of blending fruits can break down the fibre to some extent, making sugars more readily available and potentially leading to quicker increases in blood sugar compared to eating whole fruits. This doesn't mean that smoothies are unhealthy; they can still be a good source of nutrients if made with the right ingredients and not consumed in excessive quantities. They also often include other healthful ingredients like vegetables, nuts, seeds, and yoghurt, which can help mitigate the rapid sugar absorption.

Another point to consider with smoothies is the ease with which one can consume high quantities of calories. For example, you might not eat three oranges in one sitting, but it's quite easy to drink a smoothie containing as much fruit, plus additional ingredients like sweeteners or dairy products.

The best way to consume fruits is in their whole form. Eating whole fruits provides not only the sugars and flavours but also the full complement of fibre, vitamins, minerals, and other bioactive compounds that work synergistically to benefit health. The fibre in whole fruits not only helps to regulate the release of sugars into the bloodstream but also contributes to a sense of fullness, helping control appetite and potentially aiding in weight management.

Whole fruits also typically require more chewing, which can slow down the eating process and further assist with satiety and controlled energy intake. This can be particularly beneficial for those managing their weight or blood sugar levels.

Staying Hydrated

- Aim to drink around 2 litres of water per day. Water is the most effective fluid for hydration and does not contain calories, sugars, or additives. This amount might need to be adjusted based on your level of activity, the climate you live in, and your body size.
- Besides drinking water, you can also improve your hydration by eating foods high in water content. Fruits like watermelon, strawberries, and oranges, as well as vegetables like cucumber, lettuce, and celery, can contribute significantly to your daily water intake.
- Regular and zero-sugar soft drinks often contain additives and artificial sweeteners. While zero-sugar soft drinks are low in calories, the presence of artificial chemicals can be a concern for some. Instead, you might or simply infuse water with slices of fruits like lemon, lime, or cucumber for a refreshing taste without added chemicals.
- Although they provide vitamins and minerals, fruit juices and smoothies can also be high in sugars. When you do choose these options, just be aware you are choosing an indulgence over a good food decision.
- Alcohol can have multiple effects on your health. It is a diuretic, which means it can lead to increased urine production and thereby increase the risk of dehydration. Alcohol consumption can indeed disturb your sleep patterns and disrupt your gut microbiome. If you choose to drink, it's wise to do so in moderation and ensure you're also consuming plenty of water to counterbalance alcohol's dehydrating effects.

Chapter Summary & Key Points

- Hydration is essential for regulating body temperature, facilitating cellular functions, and aiding digestion

- Dehydration can cause symptoms like thirst, dark urine, dry mouth, fatigue, and headaches. Long-term effects could eventually lead to very serious conditions like hypovolemic shock.

- Alcohol is significant in social settings and rituals but has health drawbacks. It can impair liver function, affect cognitive and gut health, and increase the risk of several diseases.

- Soft drinks, high in sugar and often termed as "empty calories," pose health risks like obesity and diabetes. Alternatives like zero-sugar drinks, though lower in calories, still raise concerns.

- While juices lack fibre and can cause rapid sugar absorption, smoothies retain more fibre but can still lead to high sugar intake.

- Learn to cook. Eat less processed food, eat more veg. Drink more water.

CHAPTER 12
FERMENTED FOODS

Fermented foods have been an integral part of human diets across various cultures for thousands of years. These foods undergo a process where microorganisms such as bacteria, yeasts, or moulds break down food structures (such as sugars and starches) into other products (like alcohol or acids). This not only preserves these foods but also enhances their nutritional value, flavour, and digestibility.

The tradition of fermentation is as old as human civilization. Archaeological evidence suggests that as early as 7000 BC, societies in ancient China were fermenting beverages. Around the same time, the production of fermented milk products was taking place the area now known as Turkey. Other examples include the fermenting of vegetables in Korea, known as kimchi, and the production of miso and soy sauce in Japan. These practices were initially driven by the necessity to preserve food in a time when refrigeration did not exist, but over time they became culinary traditions that defined cultural identities.

The Science of Fermentation

Fermentation is primarily an anaerobic process that converts sugars into acids, gases, or alcohol by the action of microorganisms. It enhances food safety by lowering pH and increasing concentrations of antimicrobial compounds, inhibiting the growth of pathogenic bacteria. Different types of fermentation are driven by different microorganisms.

Lactic acid fermentation involves bacteria, primarily Lactobacillus, which is commonly found in yogurt, sauerkraut, and kefir. Ethanol fermentation by yeast is used in the making of wine, beer, and bread. Acetic acid fermentation by Acetobacter makes vinegar from wines and ciders.

What are fermented foods and how to use them

The fermentation process often results in the development of complex flavours due to the breakdown of food's natural components into new compounds like organic acids, esters, and alcohols. These chemical changes introduce a range of flavours from tangy and sour to umami and earthy, making fermented foods a favourite among chefs and food enthusiasts.

- Sauerkraut is made from fermented cabbage. It adds a vibrant acidity to dishes, cutting through richness and balancing fatty meats normally served on hot dogs, It is great on burgers, salads and as a BBQ side dish. Try it instead of coleslaw.
- Kimchi is a Korean staple and tastes both spicy and sour, with a deep, garlicky and onion flavour that complements a variety of dishes, from traditional Korean to modern fusion cuisines. Try this as a spicy side dish.
- Kefir and yogurt are fermented dairy products introduce a creamy texture and a tangy taste that can cool down spicy dishes or add tartness to smoothies and desserts.
- Miso, a paste made from fermented soybeans, is a great source of umami which is a kind of savoury earthy flavour. It adds depth and richness to soups, marinades, and glazes, enhancing flavours without overpowering them.
- Kombucha has a slightly vinegary taste, which can be used as a refreshing drink or a cocktail base, providing a unique twist to beverages making a soft drink taste almost alcoholic.
- Tempeh is like tofu block fermented from soybeans, and has a nutty flavour and firm texture, making it a substantial meat substitute in vegetarian and vegan dishes.

- Miso or fermented dairy can be whisked into sauces and dressings to introduce umami or tangy notes, enriching the overall taste of salads and entrées. The acidity of kimchi or sauerkraut can balance the richness of oily or fatty foods, making them more palatable and digestible.
- Yogurt and kefir are excellent in marinades, as their acidity helps to tenderize meats while adding flavour.
- Sourdough, which relies on natural fermentation, imparts a tangy flavour to breads that is both distinctive and flavourful, enhancing the bread's complexity.

Health Benefits

As research continues to uncover the complex interactions between fermented foods and our bodies, the potential for these foods to contribute to overall health and wellness becomes increasingly clear. Encouraging the incorporation of a variety of fermented foods into the diet may be a valuable strategy for enhancing health across multiple dimensions.

Fermented foods may influence skin health positively due to their probiotic content and the presence of bioactive peptides, vitamins, and minerals produced during the fermentation process. Chronic inflammation is a root cause of many skin issues like acne, eczema, and psoriasis. The anti-inflammatory properties of fermented foods can help alleviate these conditions. Many fermented foods have higher levels of antioxidants than their non-fermented counterparts, which can protect the skin from free radicals, reducing signs of aging and improving overall skin health.

Fermented foods and weight management is an emerging area of interest. Some studies suggest that the microbiome influences body weight, fat distribution, and metabolism. Fermented foods can contribute to a healthier microbiome, which may help in managing body weight. Fermentation can alter hormone levels involved in hunger and satiety, such as ghrelin and leptin, potentially helping to manage body weight.

The high fibre content in fermented plants-based foods can increase satiety, reducing overall calorie intake. Some probiotics found in fermented foods can enhance metabolic rate, improving fat burning and reducing storage.

Impact on gut health

The human gut microbiome consists of trillions of microorganisms, including bacteria, fungi, and viruses, all coexisting within our intestinal tract. This complex community plays a pivotal role in many physiological processes beyond digestion, including metabolic functions, immune system regulation, and even behavioural influences through the gut-brain axis (which is a big nerve running from the gut to the brain). The balance and diversity of these gut inhabitants are crucial for maintaining overall health.

Fermented foods are rich in probiotics, which are live beneficial bacteria that are introduced to the gut through consumption. These probiotics in fermented foods listed above such as yogurt, kefir, sauerkraut, and kimchi add to the microbial diversity of the gut flora. By integrating themselves into the gut ecosystem, these beneficial bacteria can help outcompete harmful pathogens, potentially reducing the risk of gastrointestinal infections and improving gut barrier functions.

A diverse gut microbiota is associated with better health outcomes. Regular consumption of a variety of fermented foods can introduce multiple strains of beneficial bacteria into the gut, each with unique roles. This increased microbial diversity helps stabilize the gut ecosystem and makes it more resilient against disturbances like infections or antibiotic use. A healthy microbiome with a diverse variety of good gut microbes can more effectively metabolise nutrients from the diet, detoxify harmful compounds, and produce essential vitamins and neurotransmitters.

Beyond influencing gut health directly, the probiotics in fermented foods interact with other physiological systems. For example, they can enhance immune function by activating certain immune cells and producing antimicrobial peptides, which protect against pathogens. The anti-inflammatory effects of probiotics can also benefit systemic health conditions like allergies, asthma, and metabolic syndrome.

Challenges

One of the main challenges with fermented foods is the inconsistency in the levels of probiotics they contain. The method and duration of fermentation can significantly impact the types and quantities of probiotics in the final product. Traditional homemade methods may differ vastly from commercial processes, leading to variability even within the same type of food.

Probiotic organisms are sensitive to environmental conditions such as temperature and pH. Improper storage can reduce their viability, diminishing the probiotic benefits of the food. Not all probiotics are the same; different strains offer different health benefits. Many fermented products do not specify which strains they contain, making it difficult for consumers to know what benefits they can expect.

While fermented foods are generally safe and healthy for most people, they can pose risks to certain groups. People with weakened immune systems may be at risk of infections from probiotics.

Fermented foods are often high in histamine, a compound produced during fermentation. People with histamine intolerance may experience allergy-like symptoms when consuming these foods. In some cases, the high levels of active cultures in fermented foods can cause bloating, gas, or digestive issues particularly for those who are not used to consuming them.

The growing popularity of fermented foods has led to an increase in commercially available products that claim to offer probiotic benefits. However, some of these claims may be misleading:

Some products labelled as "fermented" are pasteurised after fermentation, which kills the beneficial gut microbes. Unless a product specifically states it contains "live" or "active" cultures, the probiotic benefits might be minimal.

There is often a hype surrounding probiotics and fermented foods, leading some manufacturers to make exaggerated health claims that are not supported by robust scientific evidence. Many dairy products labelled "as good for your gut" can also contain a high sugar content and should be avoided.

Fermenting at home

Fermenting foods at home can be an enjoyable and rewarding process, allowing you to explore various flavours while reaping health benefits. Before you undertake the recipes at the end of this chapter read the following few paragraphs to set your fermentations up for success and make them safely.

To begin fermenting at home, you'll need a few basic tools. Spring form glass jars, which are easy to clean and fill. Glass is non-reactive and doesn't retain odours or flavours. While specialized fermentation lids that allow gases to escape are available, you can also use regular jar lids; just remember not to screw them on too tightly to allow gases to escape.

You need weights keep the vegetables submerged in brine. You can use fermentation weights, clean boiled stones, or even a smaller glass jar that fits inside the larger one. Another tip is to put a zip locked bag with some water on top of your brined vegetables to weigh them down under the water line.

A large mixing bowl is useful for preparing and mixing ingredients before they go into your fermentation jars and maybe invest in a digital weighing scales for accurately measuring salt, spices, water, and other ingredients.

When fermenting always start with clean hands, utensils, and surfaces. Sterilise all jars and tools you will use by boiling them or using a dishwasher's sterilise setting.

Keep your fermenting jars at a stable temperature, generally between 18-24°C. Extreme temperatures can inhibit fermentation or promote the growth of harmful bacteria.

Taste your ferment regularly. It should start tasting tangy or sour. If it tastes off or unpleasant, discard it. Invest in a pH tester, a good pH for a ferment to be is 4 or below.

Keep an eye out for mould. White yeast formations (kahm yeast) on the surface are generally harmless, but any coloured moulds should be taken seriously. If any mould appears, regardless of the type of mould, discard the contents of the jar.

Fermentation is not an exact science when done at home, and results can vary. Observe the changes in flavour and texture and adjust your methods as you learn what works best in your environment.

Recipe- Sauerkraut

Ingredients:

- 1 kilogram of white cabbage
- 30 grams of fine sea salt
- Optional: Spices such as caraway seeds or juniper berries for added flavour

Instructions:

Remove the outer leaves of the cabbage and set one aside for later use.

Rinse the cabbage under cold water and then dry it. Finely slice or shred the cabbage. You can use a sharp knife, a mandolin, or a food processor with a slicing attachment.

Place the shredded cabbage in a large mixing bowl. Sprinkle the salt over the cabbage. Use your hands to massage the salt into the cabbage. Squeeze the cabbage as you go; this helps to break down the cellular structure of the cabbage and release its juices.

After thoroughly mixing, let the cabbage sit for about 30 minutes to an hour. This waiting period allows the salt to further draw out moisture from the cabbage.

Transfer the cabbage into your clean jar, a handful at a time, pressing it down firmly with your fist or a tamper to pack it tightly and eliminate air pockets. This packing is crucial as it helps to submerge the cabbage under its liquid, which is vital for anaerobic fermentation.

Continue this process until the jar is filled to about three-quarters full, ensuring there is enough liquid to completely cover the cabbage. The cabbage should be submerged under its juice by at least 2 cm.

Place the whole cabbage leaf that you saved earlier over the top of the shredded cabbage. Tuck it down the sides to help keep the shredded cabbage submerged.

Place your smaller jar or fermentation weight on top to keep everything pressed down. The goal is to keep the cabbage submerged under its brine to prevent exposure to air.

Cover the mouth of the jar with a clean tea towel or muslin and secure it with a rubber band. This setup allows gases to escape while keeping contaminants out.

Leave the jar at room temperature (ideally between 18-22 degrees Celsius) and out of direct sunlight for at least 1 week. You can taste the sauerkraut after a week; if it's tangy enough for your liking, it's done. If not, let it ferment for longer. Some people prefer a fermentation period of up to 4-6 weeks for a stronger flavour.

Check the sauerkraut every few days to ensure it is still submerged in the brine. If needed, press it down to expel any trapped air and ensure it is covered by the brine.

Once fermentation is complete to your taste, replace the tea towel with a lid and store the sauerkraut in the fridge. It will keep for several months chilled.

Recipe- Kimchi

Ingredients:

- 1 kg Chinese cabbage (Napa cabbage)
- 30g sea salt
- 4 spring onions, chopped into 2-3 cm pieces
- 1 medium daikon radish (about 200g), peeled and cut into matchsticks
- 3 cloves of garlic, minced
- 20g fresh ginger, peeled and grated
- 20g sugar
- 30ml fish sauce (or you can substitute with soy sauce)
- 40g Korean chilli flakes (gochugaru)

Instructions:

Cut the cabbage in half lengthwise, then cut into 3 cm wide strips.

Place the cabbage in a large mixing bowl and sprinkle with the sea salt. Massage the salt into the cabbage until it starts to soften a bit. Then add enough water to cover the cabbage. Place a plate on top and weigh it down with something heavy. Let it sit for 1-2 hours.

While the cabbage is salting, combine the garlic, ginger, sugar, and fish sauce in a small bowl. Mix these into a paste, then add the Korean chilli flakes, mixing thoroughly until the mixture forms a smooth paste.

After the cabbage has been salting for 1-2 hours, rinse it thoroughly under cold water at least three times to remove excess salt. Allow the cabbage to drain in a colander for another 15-20 minutes.

Squeeze any remaining water from the cabbage and return it to the mixing bowl. Add the chopped spring onions and daikon radish.

Wear gloves to protect your hands from the chilli, then add the kimchi paste to the vegetables. Thoroughly mix all the ingredients, ensuring the paste evenly coats all pieces of vegetable.

Pack the kimchi into an airtight container or a jar, pressing down on it as you go to remove air pockets and ensure the vegetables are submerged in their juice.

Seal the container and let it sit at room temperature for 1-2 days for initial fermentation (you might want to open the container occasionally to let gases escape and to press down on the vegetables to keep them submerged).

After 1-2 days, taste the kimchi. If it's to your liking, transfer the container to the fridge. It will continue to ferment slowly in the fridge and will be ready to eat within a week. The flavour will continue to develop, and the kimchi will keep in the fridge for a few months.

Recipe- Yogurt

Ingredients:

- 1 litre of full fat milk
- 3-5 tablespoons of live cultured yogurt (make sure it contains live or active cultures)

Instructions:

Ensure the yogurt used as a starter is at room temperature, which helps it blend better with the milk.

Pour the milk into the saucepan and slowly heat it over medium heat. Monitor the temperature with your thermometer. You need to heat it to about 85°C. This high temperature is crucial as it alters the milk's protein structure, allowing it to set rather than curdle.

Once the milk reaches 85°C, remove it from the heat and allow it to cool to about 43°C. This is the ideal temperature for the cultures to grow and ferment the milk into yogurt.

Place the 3-5 tablespoons of live cultured yogurt into a small bowl. Add about 250 ml of the cooled milk and whisk until smooth. This helps temper the yogurt culture, making it less likely to shock when added to all the hot milk.

Pour the yogurt mixture back into the pan with the rest of the milk and whisk gently to distribute evenly. Pour the milk and yogurt mixture into your container and cover it. Place it in your chosen warm place (where the temperature is ideally around 43°C) to incubate. Leave it undisturbed for at least 6-8 hours, but preferably overnight. The longer you leave the yogurt to incubate, the thicker and tangier it will become. Some people use a insulated drinks flask for this.

After incubation, check if the yogurt has set—if it's firm and there is a small amount of liquid (whey) on the surface, it's ready. Refrigerate it for at least 4 hours to halt the fermentation process and stabilise the texture.

Once chilled, stir the yogurt if there is any whey to blend it back in for a creamier texture. Your homemade yogurt is now ready to eat. It can be enjoyed plain or with fruits, honey, or nuts for added flavour.

Always save a few tablespoons of your homemade yogurt to use as a starter for your next batch.

Add flavourings or sweeteners after the yogurt has fermented and cooled to avoid interfering with the bacterial cultures during fermentation.

Chapter Summary & Key Points

- Fermented foods have been a part of human diets for thousands of years, originating from the need to preserve foods before refrigeration existed.

- Fermentation is an anaerobic process where microorganisms like bacteria, yeasts, and moulds convert sugars and starches into acids, gases, or alcohol.

- Health Benefits: Fermented foods contribute to health by enhancing gut microbiota diversity, offering probiotics, improving skin health, and potentially aiding in weight management.

- Despite their benefits, fermented foods can vary in probiotic levels based on fermentation methods, and commercially produced fermented foods may be high in additives and sugar.

- Home fermentation is very easy to get in to, although it requires careful management of environmental conditions to ensure safety, it's the cheapest and most natural and potent way to consume probiotics.

- Learn to cook. Eat less processed food, eat more veg. Consider fermenting your vegetables first.

CHAPTER 13
GUT HEALTH

The digestive process begins in the mouth, where both mechanical and chemical digestion take place. When food enters the mouth, teeth break it down mechanically by chewing, while saliva moistens it for easier swallowing and starts the chemical breakdown of carbohydrates through enzymes. After being chewed and moistened, the food, now a soft mass called a bolus, is pushed towards the back of the mouth and into the oesophagus. The oesophagus is a muscular tube that connects the throat to the stomach. The movement of the bolus along this tube is facilitated by a series of muscular contractions.

When it reaches the stomach, the bolus is subjected to a highly acidic environment where it is further broken down by gastric acids and enzymes. The stomach churns the bolus, mixing it with digestive juices to form a semi-fluid paste called chyme.

The chyme then moves into the small intestine, which is the primary site for nutrient absorption. The small intestine is lined with tiny hair-like structures called villi and microvilli, which greatly increase the surface area for absorption. Here, digestive enzymes from the pancreas and bile from the liver aid in the breakdown of proteins, fats, and carbohydrates. Nutrients absorbed through the walls of the small intestine enter the bloodstream and are transported to cells throughout the body.

Following nutrient absorption, the remaining waste products move into the large intestine, or gut, where water and salts are absorbed, transforming the waste from liquid to solid form. The large intestine hosts a significant number of microbes that play a role in the digestive process and in maintaining gut health.

The solid waste, now called faeces, moves into the rectum, where it is stored until it is expelled from the body during defecation. This marks the end of the digestive journey.

Microbes

The role of microbes in the gut is integral not only to digestion but also to overall health and immunity. The human gut hosts a complex community of bacteria, viruses, fungi, and other microorganisms, collectively known as the gut microbiota. This ecosystem plays several crucial roles in the functioning of the body.

Although humans can digest food without the direct help of microbes, these microorganisms enhance the process. For instance, some dietary fibres cannot be digested by human enzymes and require bacterial fermentation to break them down. This fermentation process in the colon produces short-chain fatty acids (SCFAs) such as butyrate, acetate, and propionate, which are critical energy sources for our body cells, particularly colonocytes (the cells lining the colon). These SCFAs also help in absorbing minerals and managing pH levels in the gut, which prevents the growth of harmful bacteria.

Gut microbes play a crucial role in modulating inflammation within the body. Certain gut bacteria produce substances that can influence immune responses and reduce inflammation.

About 70% of the immune system is indeed associated with the gut, often referred to as the gut-associated lymphoid tissue (GALT). The GALT interacts extensively with the microbes in the gut. This interaction is crucial for the development of the immune system; microbes help train immune cells to differentiate between harmful invaders and non-threatening entities (including food and self- produced cells). By stimulating the immune system in this way, gut microbes help prepare it to fight off infections and diseases more effectively.

The source of gut microbes.

The human genome comprises about 20,000 to 25,000 genes, the microbial genome in our body is estimated to contain over 3 million genes. To put that into perspective; over 99% of the genes that you carry are not your human genes, they are the genes of the microbes that live in and on you.

These microbial genes contribute to a wide range of functions that human genes cannot perform, including certain metabolic reactions, vitamin synthesis, and the breakdown of complex dietary nutrients. This vast genetic repository provides biochemical capabilities that humans have not had to evolve on their own, suggesting a deep evolutionary connection between us and our microbiota, that live in and on us.

When a baby is born through natural childbirth, they pass through the birth canal, where they are coated with microbes from their mother. This initial exposure is crucial, as it starts the colonisation of the baby's gut, skin, and mucous membranes with beneficial bacteria. These microbes not only aid in the digestion of the mother's milk but also begin to train the baby's immune system, helping it to distinguish between harmful pathogens and harmless entities. Babies born via caesarean section (C-section) miss out on this initial natural microbial coating. Research shows that these babies may have different microbial compositions, which can be associated with a higher risk of developing allergies, asthma, and other immune-related conditions later in life.

As we grow, our environment continues to shape our microbiome. The food we eat probably has the most significant influence. Diets rich in diverse and fibrous foods, such as fruits, vegetables, and whole grains, encourage the growth of a healthy and diverse gut microbiota. On the other hand, a diet high in processed foods and sugars can promote harmful bacteria, leading to dysbiosis and associated health issues.

Living in different geographical locations, traveling, and even the people and animals we interact with contribute to the diversity of our personal microbiome. For instance, kissing someone or living with pets introduces us to new microbes that can become part of our microbiome.

Spending time in nature and engaging in activities like gardening or working the land also exposes us to a myriad of beneficial microbes. Soil is a rich source of microbial life, and regular contact with it can help enhance our microbiome's diversity. This exposure is thought to contribute to our immune system's development and its ability to manage inflammation effectively whilst also being great for our mental health in spending time outdoors.

Our sanitary world

Many aspects of contemporary life—from the way babies are born and fed to how our food is produced and how we interact with our environment—can have profound effects on our microbes therefore a profound effect on our overall health.

The increase in caesarean sections (C-sections) is one of the first modern interventions that affect microbial health. As mentioned, babies born via C-section miss out on crucial early exposure to maternal microbes that occurs during vaginal birth. This early microbial seeding is critical for developing a robust immune system and a balanced gut microbiome.

Following birth, the choice of infant nutrition further influences microbial development. Breast milk is not just a source of nutrition; it is also rich in beneficial microbes and contains prebiotics that help nourish a baby's gut microbiota. Formula milk, while a necessary option for many parents, does not provide the same microbial or prebiotic benefits. This can lead to differences in gut microbiota maturation between breastfed and formula-fed infants.

The widespread use of antibiotics has also had a significant impact. While antibiotics are invaluable for treating bacterial infections, they can indiscriminately kill beneficial bacteria along with harmful ones. Frequent or inappropriate use of antibiotics can lead to a decrease in microbial diversity and the eradication of crucial microbes, sometimes leading to long-term health consequences like increased susceptibility to infections and possibly even chronic diseases.

The way our food is produced and processed in industrial settings further contributes to the depletion of our microbiomes. Highly processed foods, often low in fibre and high in sugar and fats, do not support the diverse microbial ecosystems seen in people who consume a varied and plant-rich diet. The use of pesticides and other chemicals in farming can reduce the microbial diversity of the plants themselves and, by extension, affect the gut microbiome of those who consume them.

Living in urban environments exposes people to less microbial diversity than rural or natural settings. Urbanisation typically involves more sterile environments with fewer natural microbial interactions. The high-density living conditions can increase exposure to pathogens, sometimes leading to over-sanitisation and excessive use of disinfectants. Such practices, while necessary for controlling pathogen spread, can also diminish beneficial microbial exposures.

The heightened focus on cleanliness and sanitisation during the COVID-19 pandemic has led to an increased use of antibacterial and antiviral cleaning products. While effective at reducing the risk of virus transmission, these practices also reduce our exposure to beneficial microbes that are essential for building a good immune system.

Feeding your gut

Feeding your gut, the right way is essential for maintaining a healthy microbiome, which in turn supports overall health. In the UK and Ireland, a significant portion of the diet (as much as half the calories we consume) consists of ultra-processed foods, which can have detrimental effects on gut bacteria. These foods are designed to be digested quickly, primarily in the small intestine, leaving little to no nutrients for the beneficial microbes residing in the large intestine. The chemicals and additives often found in ultra-processed foods may potentially harm these bacteria, disrupting the delicate balance of our gut ecosystem.

In contrast, fibre-rich foods are a bit like a nourishing slow hike for your digestive system, compared to the rapid 100-meter sprint of digesting processed foods. High-fibre foods such as fruits, vegetables, legumes, and whole grains are digested more slowly, ensuring that nutrients are released gradually along the digestive tract. This slow journey allows the microbes at different stages of the gut to access and utilise these nutrients at various stages of digestion.

The fibre in these foods is not digested in the small intestine but reaches the colon where it serves as a vital food source for gut bacteria. These microbes ferment the fibre into short-chain fatty acids, which are crucial for gut health, providing energy to colon cells and helping to regulate immune function and inflammation.

A diet rich in diverse nutrients and high in fibre is particularly beneficial for nurturing the beneficial bacteria that reside in our gut. Certain food groups stand out for their gut-friendly properties, including peas, beans, legumes, fresh fruits and vegetables, nuts and seeds, and whole grains. These foods are not only rich in fibre but also packed with vitamins, minerals, and antioxidants, making them excellent choices for a gut-healthy diet.

Peas, beans, and legumes are high in both soluble and insoluble fibre, which help to regulate digestion and provide sustenance for good gut bacteria. Fresh fruits and vegetables add a variety of fibres and phytochemicals to the diet, which help to diversify the gut microbiota. Nuts and seeds, contribute healthy fats and additional fibre, while whole grains provide essential B vitamins and minerals, along with substantial amounts of fibre.

The Mediterranean diet includes a lot of legumes, whole grains, nuts, seeds, fruits, and vegetables. Dishes like Greek bean soup (fasolada), Italian minestrone (rich with beans and vegetables), and Spanish lentil stew incorporate these elements in a diet that's proven to help people live longer and healthier.

Indian food makes extensive use of legumes and pulses, including lentils, chickpeas, and various types of beans. Dishes such as dahl (a lentil stew), chana masala (spiced chickpeas), and various vegetable curries not only feature these ingredients but also include a range of spices that can further aid digestion.

Middle Eastern cuisine offers a variety of dishes that are rich in legumes, nuts, seeds, and whole grains. Hummus (made from chickpeas), tabbouleh (a bulgur wheat salad with herbs and vegetables), and falafel (fried balls made from ground chickpeas or fava beans) are all staple dishes that support a healthy gut.

Irish cuisine also offers options beneficial for gut health. Dishes like Irish stew, made with barley, and colcannon, featuring cabbage and other vegetables, incorporate whole grains and vegetables. British dishes also include lots of gut friendly ingredients like oats in porridge, marrowfat peas in pea soup and a variety of vegetables in traditional casseroles.

By prioritising real, minimally processed foods, we support a gradual, sustained release of nutrients, that nourishes our body and our good microbes throughout the day. This approach not only enhances our digestive health but also fortifies our immune system and may reduce the risk of numerous chronic diseases.

Gut Brain Axis

The gut-brain axis is a complex communication network linking the emotional and cognitive centres of the brain with the gut. It operates as a two-way street, with traffic flowing in both directions: the brain affects gut function, and the gut influences brain function.

Signals from the gut to the brain can significantly affect our mood, hunger levels, and food cravings. For example, the gut microbiota can produce neurotransmitters such as serotonin, which is known for its role in enhancing mood and general feelings of well-being. A substantial portion of the body's serotonin is produced in the gut. When this balance is disrupted, it can lead to changes in mood and emotional well-being.

The gut produces short-chain fatty acids (SCFAs) when it digests fibre. These SCFAs have several roles, including acting on the brain to regulate hunger and satiety. By influencing the release of appetite-regulating hormones like leptin and ghrelin, these fatty acids can decrease or increase hunger, respectively. The gut microbiota also interacts with the immune system, which can affect brain function and even behaviour, linking gut health closely with mental health.

Looking at the diet's impact on the gut-brain axis, the composition of the gut microbiota is highly responsive to dietary changes. For instance, a diet high in sugar can encourage the growth of sugar-loving bacteria. These bacteria can then influence our preferences by sending signals to the brain that enhance cravings for more sugary foods. Similarly, diets high in fats or salts can promote the proliferation of microbes that 'prefer' these environments, increasing cravings for these types of foods.

However, by shifting to a diet rich in plants and fibres, we cultivate a microbiota that favours the production of beneficial compounds like SCFAs. This, in turn, sends positive signals to the brain, which can reduce cravings for unhealthy foods and support overall physical and mental well-being.

We can potentially steer our diet to promote the growth of beneficial gut bacteria which can lead us to naturally prefer and crave healthier foods, increasing impact of the gut-brain relationship on our overall health.

Gut Health Issues

Poor gut health can have extensive and far-reaching effects on the entire body. The health of our gut is linked to various bodily functions, from immune responses to mental health, and maintaining a balanced gut microbiota is key to preventing many health issues.

As discussed earlier in this book, a fibre-rich diet is essential for maintaining a healthy gut microbiome. Fibre acts as a prebiotic, feeding beneficial bacteria in the large intestine and colon.

When the diet lacks sufficient fibre, the gut bacteria are deprived of their primary food source. These bacteria need to find a food source and can start to degrade the mucus layer that lines and protects the gut wall. This mucus layer is crucial as it acts as a barrier separating gut bacteria from the intestinal cells.

If the mucus layer is compromised due to being used as an alternative food source by bacteria, it can become thinner and less effective at protecting the intestinal wall. As the integrity of the mucus layer degrades, it can lead to small holes in the gut lining, commonly known as "leaky gut." This condition allows bacteria and toxins to "escape" into the bloodstream through openings in the weakened barrier.

This leakage can trigger systemic inflammation as the immune system responds to what it perceives as invaders. Such chronic inflammation can contribute to a variety of disorders, including inflammatory bowel disease (IBD) and irritable bowel syndrome (IBS). These conditions are characterised by symptoms such as pain, severe discomfort, and irregular bowel movements and can severely affect quality of life.

Since a significant part of the immune system is created in the gut, compromised gut health can lead to immune dysregulation, making the body more susceptible to infections, autoimmune diseases, and chronic inflammation.

The gut-brain axis means that gut health can directly impact mental health. For example, an unhealthy gut microbiome can affect the production of neurotransmitters such as serotonin, leading to increased risks of conditions such as depression and anxiety.

There is growing evidence linking poor gut health to various chronic conditions such as obesity, type 2 diabetes, and even heart disease, all of which can be exacerbated by systemic inflammation driven by gut dysfunction.

This reinforces the need for a diet rich in diverse fibres, along with a lifestyle that supports microbial diversity, is essential to sustain a healthy gut barrier and a balanced immune response, safeguarding not just digestive health but the health of the entire body.

Treating an unhealthy gut

Treating an unhealthy gut is an approach that considers the interactions within the gut microbiome and between the gut and other body systems. Understanding these interactions and their implications on overall health is crucial in addressing gut health issues effectively.

In some cases, individuals may be completely depleted of certain types of bacteria that perform essential functions in the gut. This can result from several factors, including prolonged antibiotic use, poor dietary habits, chronic stress, and environmental influences. The absence of these crucial bacteria can disrupt the gut's ability to process food, absorb nutrients, and regulate immune responses.

Treatment strategies involve probiotic supplementation to reintroduce beneficial bacteria into the gut. However, it's not just about adding these bacteria; it's also crucial to create an environment that supports their growth and sustenance. This is where prebiotics (fibrous foods that act as food for gut bacteria) come into play, promoting the growth of healthy bacteria. Dietary changes to include a diverse range of nutrients are vital in these circumstances and can help restore balance and function to the gut microbiome.

Humans have evolved to have a sophisticated digestive system that is closely integrated with other physiological processes, including the immune system and the brain. Our bodies have developed to listen to and interpret signals from the gut, an ability that has likely provided evolutionary advantages by helping our ancestors avoid certain diseases or toxins. Today, this system not only helps in digesting food but also in regulating our bodily functions and even our behaviour.

There is an undeniable link between mental health issues and gut health, often reflected in the symptoms of both. Conditions like anxiety and depression frequently co-occur with gastrointestinal problems such as irritable bowel syndrome (IBS), constipation, or diarrhoea. This relationship is partly explained by the gut-brain axis, which allows for constant communication between the gastrointestinal tract and the brain.

The gut-brain axis explains how a disturbance in the gut can send signals to the brain, affecting mood and emotional well-being. Conversely, stress and anxiety can lead to alterations in various digestive symptoms. Treating gut health can often alleviate some symptoms of mental health disorders, and vice versa, suggesting a holistic approach is beneficial. Since stress can significantly impact gut health, practices such as meditation, yoga, and mindfulness are often recommended, and regular exercise has also been shown to promote a healthy gut microbiome. This holistic view highlights the interconnectedness of our bodily systems and the need for integrated treatment approaches.

Incorporating a diverse range of plant-based foods to increase fibre intake, alongside reductions in processed and high-sugar foods. Using supplements can help to reintroduce and nourish beneficial gut bacteria. But long term this should be supported with a healthy diet.

Chapter Summary & Key Points

- The digestive process starts in the mouth and proceeds through the oesophagus to the stomach, through the small intestine, and ends in the large intestine which is what we call our gut. The gut microbes that live there plays a vital role in digestion, immunity, and overall health.

- The microbes' genes in our bodies outnumber human genes and contribute to many functions that our own genes do not cover, such as vitamin synthesis and the breakdown of complex nutrients.

- Diets high in processed foods can harm the gut microbiome, whereas fibrous foods like fruits, vegetables, and whole grains promote a healthy and diverse microbiome.

- Poor gut health can lead to conditions where toxins enter the bloodstream, causing inflammation and various health disorders.

- Learn to cook. Eat less processed food, eat more veg. To support your gut health.

Chapter 14
POOP!

The thing we do every day (if we are healthy) is probably the least likely topic of conversation at the dinner table but the journey of food from the mouth to its final exit is a complex and vital process for our health. In my work, when I discuss fibre and gut health, I sometimes joke about that the guidance I give is more to do with digestion than nutrition. But it is important we know how our digestion works.

The digestive process

Digestion begins in the mouth. As we chew, food is mechanically broken down and mixed with saliva. Enzymes in saliva, primarily amylase, commence the breakdown of carbohydrates, transforming them into simpler sugars.
Food then travels down the oesophagus (food pipe) into the stomach, the stomach acts like a muscular organ that further breaks down food using stomach acids and enzymes. The stomach's acidic environment initiates the digestion of proteins and churns the food into a semi-liquid form, known as chyme.

Next, the chyme enters the small intestine, where most nutrient absorption occurs. This 20-foot-long tube is lined with villi and microvilli, tiny finger-like projections that significantly increase its surface area, aiding in efficient absorption of nutrients into the bloodstream.
In the large intestine, water and electrolytes are absorbed, and the remaining material is turned into a more solid form, faeces (or poop). This organ also plays a role in storing waste until defecation.

Faeces are formed from waste products of digestion, including undigested food, bacteria, and cells shed from the

GI tract lining. The rectum stores faeces until they are expelled through the anus, completing the digestive process.

The microbiome, comprising bacteria, fungi, and viruses residing in the digestive tract, is essential in breaking down food residues, producing vitamins, and protecting against harmful pathogens. Recent research highlights the microbiome's influence on mental health, immune function, and susceptibility to diseases like obesity and diabetes.

What exactly is in poop.

About 60% of the solid matter in poop is bacteria. This might sound alarming, but it's perfectly normal. These bacteria are largely the remnants of the gut microbiota, the trillions of microorganisms living in our intestines. These tiny inhabitants play a crucial role in digestion, helping break down food and synthesize vitamins.

When we eat, we're not just feeding ourselves; we're feeding our gut bacteria too. Some of these bacteria are beneficial, aiding in digestion and supporting our immune system. Others are less helpful and can cause problems if they become too numerous. The balance of these bacterium types is crucial for our health.

As food passes through our gut, it's broken down and nutrients are absorbed. What's left – including undigested fibre, dead cells, and bacteria – forms poop. This high bacterial content is a sign of the gut's constant work and turnover.

Bowel Movements

On average, a person poops about 1.7 times per day. This figure can vary widely among individuals, influenced by factors like diet, hydration, and lifestyle. Regular bowel movements are a sign of a healthy digestive system.

The quantity of stool excreted by an average person is roughly 30 millilitres per five kilograms of body weight daily. Therefore, an average 70-kilogram person would excrete about half a kilogram of poop per day. This quantity can fluctuate based on diet, particularly the intake of fibre, which adds bulk to stool and aids in digestion.

The transit time, which is the duration it takes for food to travel from ingestion to being excreted as stool, typically ranges between 24 to 48 hours. However, this can vary significantly, from as short as 14 hours to as long as 60 hours. This variation depends on several factors, including the type of food consumed, individual metabolism, and physical activity.

The shape and size of your stool are important indicators of digestive health. Healthy poop is typically smooth and soft, shaped like a sausage or snake. Hard, lumpy, or pellet-like stool can indicate constipation, while liquid or loose stool may suggest diarrhoea or other digestive issues.

Bristol Stool Scale

The Bristol Stool Scale serves as a unique tool for understanding our bowel habits. This scale provides valuable insights into our digestive health.

The scale was developed based on a study involving 2,000 people. Participants were asked to match their bowel movements to a chart of stool types. This study helped identify common patterns in stool consistency and frequency, providing a practical way to monitor bowel health.

Essentially the Bristol Stool Scale is a tool for self-assessment of bowel health. Regular monitoring can help identify potential issues like constipation or diarrhoea, which can be early signs of dietary issues or health problems.

The Scale: Numbers and States of Matter

- Type 1: Separate hard lumps, like nuts (hard to pass) - Indicates severe constipation.
- Type 2: Sausage-shaped but lumpy - Represents mild constipation.
- Type 3: Like a sausage but with cracks on the surface - Normal and healthy.
- Type 4: Like a sausage or snake, smooth and soft - Ideal stool type.
- Type 5: Soft blobs with clear-cut edges (easy to pass) - Lacking fibre.
- Type 6: Fluffy pieces with ragged edges, a mushy stool - Slightly loose.
- Type 7: Watery, no solid pieces (entirely liquid) - Diarrhoea.

While the Bristol Stool Scale is a useful tool, it should not replace professional medical advice. If you have concerns about your bowel habits, it's always best to consult with a healthcare provider.

Sanitary Waste Management

Anyone who has ever been to a music festival can attest to the importance of good sanitary waste management. Given its composition, it's vital to manage poop and urine in a sanitary manner. In environments where sanitation is poor, such as refugee camps or regions facing humanitarian crises, the risks are significant.

Human faeces can carry pathogens – bacteria, viruses, and parasites that cause disease. If poop isn't disposed of properly, these pathogens can contaminate water supplies, food sources, and living environments. This contamination can lead to outbreaks of diseases like cholera, dysentery, and typhoid fever, which are particularly dangerous in crowded, unsanitary conditions.

Ensuring proper sanitation – toilets, sewage systems, and waste treatment facilities – is crucial in preventing the spread of disease. In crisis situations, providing safe, sanitary waste disposal is as important as supplying food and water.

Digestive Issues

Digestive issues, ranging from constipation to irregular bowel movements, are common complaints. Often, they are a direct result of our diet and lifestyle choices. One key dietary component that plays a pivotal role in our digestive health is fibre.

Dietary fibre, found in fruits, vegetables, whole grains, and legumes, is like the body's natural broom. It sweeps through our digestive tract, aiding in the formation and passage of stool.

Increasing dietary fibre is often a first-line recommendation for addressing digestive issues. Fibre adds bulk to the stool, which stimulates the intestines to contract and move the stool along. This process not only helps alleviate constipation but also ensures the regular clearing of waste from our system, which is vital for gut health.

The recommended daily intake of fibre is about 25 grams for women and 38 grams for men. Most people consume much less than this and there is no unsafe upper limit. However, its important to note that you should look to increase your uptake gradually to avoid digestive discomfort.

Increasing Fibre

While fibre is beneficial, it's crucial to approach its intake with caution. Introducing too much fibre too quickly can lead to discomfort, including bloating, gas, and cramping. This reaction occurs because the digestive system, and particularly the microbiome, needs time to adjust to the increased fibre.

It is helpful to think of your digestive system and microbiome as a muscle. Just as you wouldn't lift extremely heavy weights without proper training, you shouldn't overload your digestive system with fibre all at once. Instead, treat it like a workout routine for your gut: start with lower amounts of fibre and gradually increase the intake. This approach allows the beneficial bacteria in your gut to adjust and thrive, leading to better digestive health.

If your current diet is low in fibre, begin by adding an extra serving of fruits or vegetables each day.: Incorporate different types of fibre (soluble and insoluble) found in various plant foods for balanced benefits.

Increasing fibre without adequate water intake can lead to constipation. Water helps fibre do its job effectively. And use common sense; pay attention to how your body reacts to dietary changes and adjust accordingly.

Chapter Summary & Key Points

- Digestion is a complex process that begins in the mouth with the mechanical breakdown and enzymatic digestion of food, continuing through the stomach and intestines, where nutrients are absorbed, and waste is eventually formed into faeces.

- Faeces primarily consist of bacteria undigested food, cells shed from the GI tract, and fibre. The composition and health of the gut microbiota are essential for effective digestion and the prevention of diseases.

- Bowel movement frequency averages around 1.7 times per day, with variations based on diet, hydration, and lifestyle.
- The Bristol Stool Scale is a diagnostic tool that classifies stool. Ideally you want to be on type 3 or 4 of this scale (like a sausage with or without cracks)

- Gradually increasing fibre intake while ensuring adequate water consumption is recommended to ensure good digestion and avoid discomfort and promote gut health.

- Learn to cook. Eat less processed food, eat more veg to avoid digestive issues.

CHAPTER 15
WEIGHT MANAGEMENT

The concept of weight loss often summed up with "calories in, calories out," suggesting that the balance between calories consumed and expended is the sole determinant of weight change. However, modern nutritional science offers a different perspective, indicating that sustainable weight management hinges on not just how much we eat, but what we eat.

The limitations of calorie counting, is that it's based on the principle that to lose weight, you must consume fewer calories than you expend. While this method can and probably will produce short-term results, it oversimplifies the complexities of our metabolism and the diverse effects of different foods on our bodies.

Recent research suggests that the type of calories consumed can influence how full you feel, metabolic rate, and even the hormonal responses to eating. Foods with a high glycaemic index, such as refined sugars and white bread, can spike insulin levels and lead to increased fat storage, compared to more nutrient-dense, lower-glycaemic options like vegetables and whole grains. Calorie counting does not account for the nutritional value of food, potentially leading to diets lacking in vitamins, minerals, and fibre, which are crucial for overall health and vital for managing weight in a sustainable way.

Its ok to look "Normal".

Every individual has a unique body shape and size influenced by a combination of genetics, lifestyle, and environmental factors. This diversity is perfectly normal and should be celebrated. Throughout a person's life, their body naturally changes in response to various stages of growth, development, and aging. For example, during childhood and adolescence, the body undergoes significant growth spurts and hormonal changes that shape our physique. In adulthood, factors such as career, stress, and family life can influence body weight and composition. As we age, metabolic rates slow down, and it becomes easier to gain weight, especially around the midsection. This weight gain is a natural part of the aging process and is influenced by hormonal shifts, decreased muscle mass, and changes in activity levels.

The issue is, body image is heavily influenced by social media, where doctored and filtered images create unrealistic standards of beauty. These images can distort our perception of what a healthy body looks like, leading to unrealistic expectations and negative self-esteem. It's important to recognise that these images are often not reflective of reality and that each person's healthy body looks different.

The primary goal of maintaining a healthy diet and staying active should be to support overall well-being, rather than achieving a specific appearance. Proper nutrition provides the body with essential nutrients that fuel bodily functions, support mental health, and reduce the risk of chronic diseases. Regular physical activity strengthens muscles and bones, improves cardiovascular health, and boosts mood and energy levels.

Focusing on how our bodies feel and function rather than how they look helps promote a healthier and more sustainable approach to wellness. This perspective encourages self-compassion and body positivity, recognising that health is multifaceted and personal. Eating a balanced diet rich in fruits, vegetables, whole grains, lean proteins, and healthy fats, combined with regular exercise, is the best way to ensure that our bodies operate efficiently and remain resilient throughout life.

Basal Metabolic Rate

Basal or base metabolic rate (BMR) is the amount of energy, expressed in calories, that a person needs to maintain basic bodily functions at rest. This includes processes like breathing, circulating blood, and cell production. BMR accounts for the largest portion of a person's total energy expenditure, typically around 60-75%, depending on factors such as age, sex, body composition, and genetic predisposition.

The importance of BMR in weight management is significant, as it sets the baseline for how many calories you need to consume to maintain current body weight without additional physical activity. When considering the impact of food on BMR, the concept of the thermic effect of food (TEF) comes into play. TEF refers to the energy expended by our bodies to digest, absorb, and metabolise food. Not all foods are equal in this respect; some require more energy than others to be broken down, which can subtly influence our overall energy expenditure.

Protein-rich foods, for example, have a higher thermic effect than fats or carbohydrates. This means that the body uses more calories to process proteins compared to other macronutrients. This higher thermic effect can contribute to a slightly increased rate of metabolism overall, which is beneficial for weight management. Foods high in fibre also have a similar effect. Fibre is not easily digested by the body, so consuming foods rich in dietary fibre can enhance the energy used during digestion.

Incorporating foods that are harder to digest and thus have a higher thermic effect can be a useful strategy in weight management. It not only supports a higher metabolic rate but also contributes to feelings of fullness, which can help in reducing overall calorie intake. However, it's important to maintain a balanced approach; while choosing foods based on their thermic effect can aid in managing body weight, the overall nutritional balance of the diet should not be overlooked.

In essence, the goal is not just to count calories but to choose foods that boost metabolism naturally, aligning your body's basal metabolic needs with dietary intake for more effective weight management.

Eat more to manage your weight!

Eating more to lose weight may sound counterintuitive, but when done correctly, it can be an effective approach to weight management. This strategy hinges on the principle of consuming foods that are rich in nutrients, take longer to digest and tend to be lower in calories. This way of eating not only satisfies hunger but also nourishes the body, supporting healthy weight loss and maintenance.

A nutrient-rich, high-fibre diet plays a crucial role in keeping you fuller for longer. High-fibre foods like fruits, vegetables, legumes, and whole grains have a lower energy density, which means they provide fewer calories relative to their weight. Fibre adds bulk to your diet without adding extra calories, slowing down the digestion process, which in turn helps to maintain steady blood sugar levels and keep you feeling fuller for longer. This prolonged feeling of fullness helps to naturally reduce the amount of food consumed throughout the day, thereby aiding in weight management.

On the other hand, refined carbohydrates and ultra-processed foods are a hindrance on effective weight management. These foods are often high in calories and low in nutrients. They are quickly digested, leading to rapid spikes and subsequent drops in blood sugar levels, which can result in frequent hunger pangs and cravings. Foods such as white bread, pastries, and sugary snacks lack dietary fibre and essential nutrients, which makes them less filling and more likely to contribute to overeating.

A diet that focuses on filling your plate with nutrient-dense, colourful foods from diverse plant sources, nutrient-rich dairy like yogurts, and polyphenol-rich herbs and spices not only provides essential vitamins, minerals, and antioxidants but also enhances the overall appeal and palatability of meals. Colourful vegetables and fruits, for instance, are not just visually appealing; their colours represent a variety of nutrients and antioxidants that can help reduce inflammation and improve metabolic health.

Choosing a variety of herbs and spices not only adds flavour without extra calories but also can contribute to better health. Many herbs and spices are rich in polyphenols, which are compounds that have antioxidant properties and can help fight inflammation. Turmeric, for example, contains curcumin, a compound with strong anti-inflammatory and antioxidant effects. Similarly, cinnamon can help in managing blood sugar levels, making it beneficial for weight loss and metabolic health.

Choosing dairy products like yogurt in your diet adds another layer of nutritional value. Yogurts, especially those that are low in sugar and high in live cultures, can improve gut health due to their probiotic content, which is essential for digestion and overall well-being. A healthy gut can significantly enhance your body's ability to absorb nutrients effectively and regulate body weight.

Activity

Maintaining a healthy weight is as much about the quality and quantity of food we eat as it is about our level of physical activity. Regular exercise is fundamental to managing weight effectively, boosting metabolism, and enhancing overall health. Health guidelines suggest that adults should aim to be active daily and accumulate at least 150 minutes of moderate aerobic activity, such as cycling or brisk walking, every week, or commit to 75 minutes of vigorous activity, such as running or sports, spread across the week. This not only supports physical health but also improves mental well-being. Exercising moderately for at least 30 minutes on a minimum five days a week or engaging in intense activity for around 25 minutes on three days a week, offers considerable health benefits. These range from improved cardiovascular fitness and bone health to significant contributions toward calorie expenditure and muscle strengthening. Structuring workouts to fit personal schedules and capabilities can make this essential physical activity a sustainable and enjoyable part of everyday life.

There are added benefits when exercise is taken outdoors, particularly in natural settings like parks, forests, or along coastlines. Exercising in nature not only elevates physical well-being through activity but also enhances mental health by reducing stress, anxiety, and depression. Natural light boosts vitamin D levels, which is crucial for bone health and immune function. Environments that engage and stimulate the mind may lead to longer, more enjoyable, and more frequent exercise sessions, thereby increasing the likelihood of sticking to a regular exercise schedule.

A newer approach gaining popularity is cold water immersion, whether it's a dip in the sea or an ice bath. Proponents believe that exposing the body to cold water can boost calorie burn by increasing metabolic rate as the body works harder to maintain its core temperature. Although still under scientific review, early research indicates potential benefits such as improved circulation, reduced muscle inflammation, and an enhanced immune response. Cold water immersion might also increase brown fat activity, a type of fat that burns off more calories than ordinary fat. This trend is reflective of a broader shift towards more varied and holistic approaches to fitness and health, combining traditional exercise with newer methodologies that offer fresh challenges and benefits.

Incorporating these elements into a routine does not require drastic changes but a commitment to explore and adapt new habits that improve health. Whether it's a brisk walk, a jog along a scenic route, or even the chill of an ice bath, the key to sustainable weight management lies in finding enjoyable, feasible, and health-promoting activities that fit into your lifestyle. Engaging in regular physical activity, particularly in invigorating and natural environments, can provide a solid foundation for not only managing weight but also for achieving a higher quality of life.

Chapter Summary & Key Points

- Its ok not to look perfect. There is no such thing as the perfect body, chances are if you eat well and exercise regularly you are the "normal" body shape that your supposed to be.

- Weight loss is not about consuming fewer calories than expended; it's about consuming the right foods in abundance. A diet high in fibre and nutrients helps feelings of fullness and manage hunger, leading to natural calorie control.

- Basal Metabolic Rate is crucial in weight management as it represents the energy needed for basic bodily functions at rest. Consuming foods with a high thermic effect can increase overall energy expenditure and aid weight management.

- Regular physical activity, whether moderate or physical, is essential for effective weight management and overall health.

- Physical activity not only improves physical health but also mental well-being, making it easier to maintain a healthy lifestyle.

- If you do wish to manage your weight better the first thing you need to do is learn to cook. Eat less processed food and eat more veg.

CHAPTER 16
FASTING

Fasting is the voluntary abstinence from food, and sometimes drink, for a specific period. It can be done for health, religious, or ethical reasons.

The history of fasting dates to ancient civilisations. Greek scholars were documented to fast for prolonged periods to purify the mind or just for health and well-being. In ancient Egypt, fasting was a common practice to prepare for religious ceremonies. In Ireland, traditionally, fasting is observed during Lent, a period of 40 days leading up to Easter, usually just for 24 hours as part of charity initiatives or Good Friday. Muslims observe fasting during the month of Ramadan, refraining from eating and drinking from dawn until sunset to cultivate self-discipline and empathy for the less fortunate.

In current times, fasting has gained popularity for its potential health benefits. Intermittent fasting, where individuals alternate between periods of eating and fasting, has been studied for its effects on weight loss, metabolism, and overall health. Some research suggests that fasting can improve insulin sensitivity, reduce inflammation, and promote cellular repair processes like autophagy.

Autophagy is a natural process by which the body cleans out damaged cells and regenerates new, healthier cells. It involves the degradation and recycling of cellular components, helping to maintain cellular health and function. During autophagy, cells break down their own components into their basic building blocks, which can then be reused for cellular repair and growth.

Types of Fasting

Fasting, when done correctly, can be a powerful tool for improving overall health and well-being, but it is not a one-size-fits-all solution. Each method has its pros and cons, and understanding these can help tailor the approach to individual goals and circumstances.

Intermittent fasting involves cycling between periods of eating and fasting. Common methods include the 16/8 method (fasting for 16 hours and eating during an 8-hour window) and the 5:2 method (eating normally for five days and consuming a very low-calorie diet for two non-consecutive days). Research suggests intermittent fasting can improve metabolic health, aid in weight loss, and enhance cognitive function by promoting cellular repair processes and reducing inflammation.

Water fasting is abstaining from all foods and consuming only water. Typically lasting 24-72 hours, this fast can help reset the digestive system and promote autophagy, a process where the body cleans out damaged cells and regenerates new ones. However, extended water fasting should be approached cautiously and under medical supervision to avoid dehydration, nutrient deficiencies, and other potential risks.

Juice fasting involves consuming only fruit and vegetable juices for a set period, usually lasting from a day to a week. This type of fast aims to provide a break for the digestive system while supplying some essential vitamins and minerals. Juice fasting can help with detoxification, improve digestion, and boost overall vitality. However, if fasting like this is severely lacking protein and fibre, making it unsuitable for long-term use.

Prolonged fasting extends beyond 48-72 hours and can last several days or even weeks. There is evidence to support health benefits from this, such as enhanced stages of autophagy, improved insulin sensitivity, and potentially even increased longevity. However, it requires careful planning and medical oversight to ensure safety and prevent adverse effects like muscle loss, electrolyte imbalances, and other health issues.

Intermittent fasting, time-restricted eating, or periodic prolonged fasting can all potentially increase the levels and activity of Akkermansia muciniphila, a beneficial gut microbe. This bacterium is important for gut health because it breaks down mucin, the main component of mucus, which helps keep the protective mucus layer of the gut intact. It also produces short-chain fatty acids (SCFAs) (such as acetate and propionate), which have anti-inflammatory properties and provide energy to cells in the colon and it regulates immune responses, helping to maintain a balanced immune system. This bacterium performs these tasks best when you are not digesting food so by giving it time to perform its functions your gut health benefits.

Fasting and Mental Health

Fasting can have significant effects on mood, which may vary depending on the type and duration of fasting. Short-term fasting, such as intermittent fasting, has been linked to improved mood and a reduction in symptoms of depression and anxiety. This effect is thought to be mediated by several mechanisms, including increased production of brain-derived neurotrophic factor, which supports brain health and resilience to stress. Additionally, fasting can enhance the production of endorphins, often referred to as "feel-good" hormones, leading to a sense of euphoria and well-being.

Research suggests that fasting can have a positive impact on cognitive function. Intermittent fasting has been shown in some cases to improve various aspects of cognitive performance, including memory, learning, and overall mental sharpness. This improvement is attributed to the growth of new neurons, particularly in the hippocampus, a brain region crucial for learning and memory. Fasting helps reduce oxidative damage to brain cells, protecting them from age-related cognitive decline. Better insulin sensitivity can lead to more stable blood sugar levels, providing a consistent energy supply to the brain.

Many individuals who practice fasting report experiencing heightened mental clarity and improved focus. This phenomenon is often linked to the metabolic switch that occurs during fasting, where the body shifts from using glucose as its primary energy source to burning fat and producing ketones. This is what the Keto Diet is based on. Ketones are a more efficient and steady fuel for the brain, this may be the reason for reported enhanced mental clarity and sustained concentration after fasting.

However, it is important to note that the initial phase of fasting can sometimes lead to irritability, mood swings, and fatigue as the body adjusts to a new eating pattern. These effects are usually temporary and tend to subside as the body becomes accustomed to fasting.

Precautions and Risks

For all the potential benefits of fasting, it also carries potential downsides and is not suitable for everyone. Understanding these risks and knowing how to fast safely is crucial. One potential downside of fasting is the risk of nutrient deficiencies. Prolonged fasting can lead to deficiencies in essential nutrients such as vitamins, minerals, and proteins, which can compromise immune function, muscle mass, and overall health. Another concern is electrolyte imbalance. Extended fasting, especially without proper hydration, can cause an imbalance in electrolytes such as sodium, potassium, and magnesium, leading to serious health issues. Blood sugar issues are another risk, particularly for people with diabetes or hypoglycaemia, who may experience dangerous drops in blood sugar levels during fasting, causing dizziness, confusion, and fainting.

Fasting can also increase the production of cortisol, the stress hormone, potentially exacerbating anxiety and stress levels. For some individuals, fasting can trigger unhealthy relationships with food, including binge eating, orthorexia, or other eating disorders. Additionally, sudden changes in eating patterns can cause digestive issues such as constipation, bloating, and indigestion.

Some groups of people should avoid fasting altogether. Pregnant and breastfeeding women have higher nutritional needs, and fasting can compromise the health of both mother and baby. Children and adolescents, who need consistent nutrition for growth and development, should also avoid fasting. Individuals with a history of eating disorders, such as anorexia or bulimia, should steer clear of fasting as it can trigger relapse or worsen symptoms. People with chronic illnesses like diabetes or heart disease, or those undergoing and health treatment, should consult healthcare providers before considering fasting. Older adults may have different nutritional requirements and health conditions that make fasting unsafe.

To fast safely, it is essential to consult with a healthcare professional before starting any fasting regimen, especially if you have pre-existing health conditions. Staying hydrated by drinking plenty of water and considering electrolytes is crucial to maintain hydration and balance in the body. Choosing the right type of fast is also important. Intermittent fasting, such as the 16/8 method, can be less extreme and more manageable than prolonged fasting. Starting with shorter fasting periods and gradually increasing as tolerated can help.

Fasting is not a replacement for a healthy diet. At all times ensure your meals are rich in essential nutrients, focusing on whole foods like fruits, vegetables, lean proteins, and whole grains. It is vital to listen to your body and pay attention to signs of distress such as dizziness, fatigue, or extreme hunger.

If you feel unwell, break the fast. Combining fasting with other healthy lifestyle practices, such as regular physical activity, adequate sleep, and stress management techniques, can contribute to a balanced approach to health.

My experience with fasting extends only up to the 36-hour mark, and to be honest, I found it easier than I initially thought. The trick lies in timing it so that you sleep through a significant portion of the fast. For instance, if your last meal is at 8 p.m. on a Saturday, you wake up on Sunday and sustain yourself with plenty of water, herbal teas, and black coffee throughout the day. By the time Sunday evening arrives, you head off to bed, and upon waking up at 8 a.m. on Monday, you can enjoy your breakfast. This approach makes it feel as though you've only fasted for a single day, even though two nights' sleep have extended the fasting period.

During this time, I did experience some light-headedness, which was after consuming caffeine in the black coffee. As a result, I would caution anyone considering this method to moderate their caffeine intake. This has been my personal experience, and I fully acknowledge that fasting can vary greatly from person to person. While this method worked for me, others might find it considerably more challenging.

Breaking a Fast

Breaking a fast (which is where the work Breakfast comes from) requires careful consideration to avoid digestive issues and to maximise the benefits of fasting. It is important to start with hydration by drinking water, herbal teas, or broths to rehydrate your body, which gently wakes up your digestive system. Initially, eat small portions as your digestive system needs time to adjust to processing food again.

Choose easily digestible foods to begin with, such as fruits, vegetables, and light soups. Bananas, melons, berries, steamed vegetables, and clear broths are the best choices. Choose low-fibre and low-fat foods initially to avoid overwhelming your digestive system, as high-fibre foods can be hard to digest after a fast, and fatty foods can cause discomfort and bloating.

Gradually reintroduce more complex foods. After starting with fruits and vegetables, move on to lean proteins like chicken, fish, and eggs, and then to whole grains and legumes. Avoid foods high in sugar and highly processed foods, as they can cause a rapid spike in blood sugar and lead to digestive discomfort. Take your time and chew your food thoroughly to aid digestion, breaking down food particles and making it easier for your digestive system to process them.

Pay attention to how your body responds to different foods and adjust your diet accordingly if you experience discomfort, introducing new foods more slowly if necessary. Continue to drink plenty of water throughout the refeeding process, as proper hydration is essential for digestion and overall health.

Incorporating probiotics and fermented foods, such as yoghurt, kefir, sauerkraut, and kimchi, can help replenish beneficial gut bacteria and aid digestion. Aim for balanced meals that include a mix of colourful carbs like fruits and vegetables, lean proteins, and good fats to ensure you are getting a range of nutrients necessary for recovery and overall health. Establish regular mealtimes to help your body get back into a routine, which can aid in normalising hunger signals and digestion.

Approach breaking a fast with care to avoid digestive issues and ensure a smooth transition back to regular eating habits. By following these best practices, you can reintroduce food in a way that uses the fast as a reset to build upon with a great nutrient dense diet.

Chapter Summary & Key Points

- Fasting involves voluntarily abstaining from food and sometimes drink for health, religious, or ethical reasons.

- Intermittent fasting, such as the 16/8 and 5:2 methods, has gained popularity for its both their physical and mental health benefits.

- Types of fasting include water fasting, juice fasting, and prolonged fasting, each with specific benefits, but they require medical supervision to avoid risks like nutrient deficiencies and electrolyte imbalances.

- Fasting can positively impact mental health by improving mood and cognitive function, but it may initially cause irritability and fatigue. It reportedly promotes mental clarity by shifting the body's energy source from glucose to ketones.

- Fasting is unsuitable for certain groups, including pregnant women, children, and individuals with eating disorders or chronic illnesses. Safe fasting requires professional consultation, proper hydration, and a gradual approach.

- After fasting eat less processed food and eat more veg.

CHAPTER 17
SLEEP

Sleep is an essential component of overall well-being, significantly impacting not just our energy levels and mood but also our dietary habits. Poor sleep can disrupt hormonal balances which regulate hunger, influencing our food choices and calorie intake.

The impact of sleep on hunger hormones

Leptin and ghrelin are hormones that play crucial roles in regulating appetite. Leptin is known as the "satiety hormone" and is produced by fat cells. It helps to regulate energy balance by inhibiting hunger, which in turn helps to regulate body weight. Under normal conditions, higher levels of leptin signal to the brain that the body has enough energy stores, suppressing your appetite.

On the other hand, ghrelin, often called the "hunger hormone," is produced in the stomach and stimulates appetite. It signals the brain when it's time to eat and promotes fat storage.

Sleep deprivation disrupts the normal production of these hormones. Research shows that when we don't get enough sleep, leptin levels drop, meaning we do not feel as satisfied after eating. Simultaneously, ghrelin levels increase, which increases our appetite. This double impact makes us feel hungrier and may lead to increased calorie consumption.

The hormonal imbalance caused by lack of sleep leads to more than just increased hunger. It also messes with the brain's reward systems, particularly the hedonic centres responsible for pleasure and satisfaction. Sleep-deprived individuals are more likely to crave sugary, salty, and high-fat comfort foods. These cravings are like those experienced by people when they have the "munchies" after consuming cannabis, due to the activation of the same pathways in the brain that enhance the pleasure of eating.

Nutrition for Sleep

Macronutrients: carbohydrates, proteins, and fats, not only fuel our daily activities but also influence sleep patterns and quality. Carbohydrates have a notable impact on sleep, primarily through their influence on the brain's levels of tryptophan, an amino acid that serves as a precursor to the neurotransmitter serotonin and the hormone melatonin. These chemicals are critical for the regulation of sleep. Consuming carbohydrates can increase insulin release, which in turn reduces the concentration of amino acids that compete with tryptophan for transport into the brain, in theory allowing more tryptophan to enter the brain and be converted into serotonin and melatonin. This could be why you feel sluggish after carb heavy meals like pasta or a baked potato.

Complex carbohydrates, such as whole grains and legumes, promote a steady rise in blood sugar levels, which supports a gradual release of insulin. On the other hand, simple carbohydrates, found in sugary snacks and drinks, cause a rapid spike in insulin and blood sugar levels, which can disrupt sleep patterns. Therefore, for those looking to improve their sleep quality, incorporating whole grains and other complex carbohydrates into their evening meals might be beneficial.

High-protein diets have been promoted for their weight loss benefits and ability to increase feeling full but their impact on sleep is less straightforward. Proteins are rich in amino acids like tyrosine, which can enhance alertness and, in some cases, counteract sleep. Broadly, research suggests that while a moderate intake of protein can be beneficial for sleep, especially due to its role in muscle repair and growth, excessive protein, particularly before bedtime, may reduce the production of serotonin in the brain, due to the lower availability of tryptophan. Incorporating a moderate amount of protein throughout the day rather than in large amounts in the evening could potentially enhance sleep quality without compromising dietary needs.

Emerging research has shed light on the significant role of gut health in sleep regulation. The gut microbiome, which comprises trillions of bacteria, not only affects digestion and immune function but also has a profound impact on the production of neurotransmitters and hormones, including those involved in sleep.

Gut bacteria produce a wide variety of neurotransmitters, such as serotonin and gamma-aminobutyric acid (GABA), which play direct roles in mood regulation and sleep. A healthy, balanced gut microbiome, therefore, can support the production of these neurotransmitters, potentially improving sleep. Conversely, an imbalance in gut bacteria may lead to disturbances in neurotransmitter levels, contributing to sleep disorders.

Dietary choices significantly influence gut health. A diet rich in diverse fibres from fruits, vegetables, whole grains, and legumes can promote a healthy gut microbiome. Fermented foods such as yogurt, kefir, and sauerkraut, which contain probiotics, are also beneficial in maintaining or restoring a healthy gut balance.

Certain foods are known to promote better sleep due to their nutritional content, particularly those rich in compounds that influence sleep-regulating hormones and neurotransmitters.

- Turkey is often associated with sleepiness, which is evident due to the need to nap after a large Christmas dinner, this is due to its high tryptophan content.
- Cherries, especially tart cherries, are one of the few natural food sources of melatonin, the hormone that regulates the sleep-wake cycle. Consuming tart cherry juice has been

shown to improve sleep duration and quality by increasing melatonin levels.
- Many nuts, such as almonds and walnuts, are good sources of magnesium and melatonin. Magnesium helps promote relaxation and sleep by supporting neurotransmitter function, while the melatonin in walnuts assists in regulating the sleep cycle. Fish like salmon, mackerel, and trout are rich in omega-3 fatty acids and vitamin D. Omega-3s increase the production of serotonin, a precursor to melatonin, while vitamin D has been linked to a longer sleep duration. Together, they can improve the quality of sleep.
- Consuming kiwis on a regular basis is linked to improvements in sleep onset, duration, and efficiency in adults, likely due to their high content of antioxidants and serotonin. Bananas are a great source of potassium and magnesium, both of which serve as muscle relaxants. They also contain tryptophan, which is converted into serotonin and melatonin in the brain, aiding in sleep.
- Milk, yogurt, and cheese also contain tryptophan. The calcium in dairy helps the brain use the tryptophan to manufacture melatonin. Additionally, consuming dairy may have a psychological link to calming routines before bed, like drinking a warm glass of milk.
- Finally, chamomile is known for its calming effects due to the antioxidant apigenin, which binds to certain receptors in the brain that may promote sleepiness and reduce insomnia.

These foods, due to their specific components and nutrients, help enhance the quality of sleep by influencing various physiological processes that regulate sleep patterns. Incorporating them into your diet can be a natural way to improve sleep.

Alcohol and sleep

Alcohol is often consumed by many seeking to unwind at the end of the day. While it may initially act as a sedative, facilitating the onset of sleep, its overall effect on sleep quality and architecture is largely disruptive, particularly to REM sleep.

Initially, alcohol can reduce the time it takes to fall asleep due to its sedative effects. As a central nervous system depressant, it slows down brain activity, making it easier to fall asleep by reducing feelings of stress and anxiety, common culprits behind insomnia. This sedative effect is why some people believe that having a drink before bed helps them sleep better.

However, despite the initial sedation, alcohol disrupts sleep architecture—the natural progression through the various stages of sleep, including REM sleep.

REM sleep, or Rapid Eye Movement sleep, is a critical stage of the sleep cycle associated with dreaming, memory consolidation, and emotional processing. Alcohol significantly reduces REM sleep during the first part of the night, leading to a rebound effect in the second part of the night. This rebound can cause unusually long and frequent REM periods, disrupting the normal sleep cycle. Since REM sleep is linked to learning and memory, reduced REM can impair cognitive function, affecting concentration and memory. Because REM sleep plays such a big a role in emotional health, insufficient REM sleep can increase susceptibility to mood disorders such as depression or anxiety.

As the body metabolises alcohol, its sedative effects wear off, leading to fragmented sleep. This means more frequent awakenings and difficulty returning to sleep, reducing sleep quality and duration, and making sleep less restorative.

Supporting a good night's sleep

Supporting a good night's sleep extends beyond cautious dietary choices to include optimising your sleep environment and evening habits.

Consuming foods and drinks that disrupt sleep quality—such as caffeine, heavy meals, spicy foods, sugary snacks, and refined carbohydrates—can have detrimental effects, making it crucial to choose your evening intake wisely. Caffeine, the stimulant found in coffee, tea, chocolate, and many soft drinks, can delay the body's internal clock and shorten sleep duration, especially if consumed late in the day. It's a good idea to avoid coffee after lunchtime and not drink more than two or three cups a day.

Heavy meals loaded with fats or spices can cause indigestion and discomfort, while spicy foods may lead to heartburn and increased body temperature, both disruptive to sleep.

To further support a restful night, it's beneficial to create a conducive sleep environment. Making your sleeping area as dark as possible can significantly enhance your sleep quality, as darkness signals to the body that it's time to wind down.

Lowering your body temperature slightly before bedtime can also promote faster sleep onset. This can be achieved by taking a warm bath or shower earlier in the evening, which helps to cool the body down by the time you go to bed. Additionally, minimising potential disturbances such as keeping your phone away from your bedside can prevent sleep disruptions from notifications and reduce the temptation to use stimulating devices right before sleep.

Chapter Summary & Key Points

- Poor sleep affects the balance of hunger-regulating hormones like leptin and ghrelin. Sleep deprivation can lower leptin levels and raise ghrelin levels, leading to increased hunger and calorie intake.

- The consumption of good balanced diet impacts sleep quality.

- A healthy gut microbiome influences the production of neurotransmitters which are crucial for mood regulation and sleep.

- Certain foods can enhance sleep quality due to their content of sleep-regulating compounds. For instance, turkey is high in tryptophan and melatonin which aid a good night sleep.

- Alcohol, while initially sedative, disrupts sleep architecture, particularly REM sleep, leading to fragmented sleep and reduced sleep quality. This disruption impacts cognitive functions and emotional health due.

- Learn to cook. Eat less processed food, eat more veg.

CHAPTER 18
HOW TO EAT

In a busy working life, I find that most of the meals I consume often resemble a race against time. I based my career in the industry of people taking time to enjoy fresh prepared food, but the reality is I rarely practice what I preach due to my perceived time pressures or simply trying to multitask eating with another thing on my to do list like office work or driving.

Mindful eating

Mindful eating is a practice that involves paying full attention to the experience of eating and drinking, both inside and outside the body. It is rooted in the Buddhist concept of mindfulness, which is a form of meditation. The essence of mindful eating is to create a deeper connection with the act of eating, transforming it into a rich, sensory exercise.

The benefits of eating slowly begin with improved digestion. When you eat at a slower pace, you allow your body to process food more efficiently, leading to better nutrient absorption and fewer digestive issues. This steady, methodical approach to eating also helps with weight management. By eating slowly, you give your body time to recognise fullness cues, preventing overeating and aiding in weight loss or maintenance. In contrast, speedy eating can lead to the opposite: poor digestion, overeating, and subsequent weight gain.

Adopting a slow eating approach isn't just about chewing your food longer; it's about creating a mindful relationship with your meals. When you eat slowly, you're likely to find more satisfaction in your meals, regardless of how simple they are. This mindful approach allows you to savour each bite, appreciate the flavours, and leave the table feeling content both physically and emotionally.

Despite these benefits, many of us consume our "western diet" too quickly, often due to our busy lifestyles. This hurried eating isn't selective; it affects everyone, from healthcare experts to everyday individuals. Studies have shown that slow eaters consume food more thoughtfully, leading to better digestion and fewer calories. People who eat slowly tend to drink more water during meals, leading to better hydration. Fast eating, on the other hand, is linked to negative outcomes like weight gain and a sense of loss of control overeating habits. Rapid eating is a common trait in disordered eating patterns, including binge eating. Slowing down can be a simple yet effective tool to regain control during episodes of compulsive or emotional eating. People who eat too fast don't give their body time to release satiety signals to the brain, often consuming up to 30% more calories per meal than people who eat more slowly.

Mindful eating is a great tool to break this cycle and use eating as a meditative practice. This practice involves being fully attentive to your food, as well as your hunger and fullness cues. This includes recognising the colours, smells, textures, flavours, temperatures, and even the sounds (like crunching) of your food. Focusing on the present moment while eating, without distraction, is crucial. This means eating without engaging in other activities like watching TV or using a smartphone.

Mindful eating also involves paying attention to physical hunger and satiety signals to guide decisions about when to begin and stop eating. This means eating because you are hungry, not because you are bored, stressed, or responding to another emotional need. The practice also involves accepting and enjoying food without labelling it as "good" or "bad". This approach helps reduce guilt and anxiety around eating, promoting a healthier relationship with food.

How to practise mindful eating

- Find a comfortable seat and make sure your feet are flat on the ground. Sit up straight to prepare yourself for a mindful eating experience.
- Take a moment to focus on your breathing. Notice if it is fast or slow. Your breath helps you stay in the present moment.
- Hold your snack and take a moment to feel it in your hand. Is it rough or smooth? Cold or warm? Paying attention to these details is an important part of mindful eating.
- Think about where your food came from. Notice its colour and shape. These are often overlooked but are important details.
- Bring the food close and smell it. Does the aroma bring back any memories or feelings? Smell is a big part of how we experience food.
- Take a bite and keep paying attention to your breathing. Notice the flavours. Which ones stand out? Are there any secondary flavours that follow? How does the size and shape of the food affect its flavour?
- There is no need to rush. Savour each bite of food. How does the taste compare to the smell? Chew slowly and think about each flavour.
- As you continue eating, stay in the moment. How does the food feel in your mouth? How does the taste change as you eat more? Describe this experience to yourself.
- After finishing your meal, take a moment to reflect. How does your body feel now? Do you notice any signs of fullness or satisfaction? Think about the meal's taste and how it met your expectations. Reflect on the textures, tastes, and aromas you experienced and how they contributed to your satisfaction. This helps you connect the physical sensations of fullness and satisfaction with the mental and emotional aspects of eating.

By acknowledging these sensations, you foster a healthier, more intuitive relationship with food.

Practising mindful eating at every meal is not always practical due to our busy schedules and social settings. However, try engaging in this practice whenever possible, especially when you are eating alone. You might be surprised by how much less you eat compared to mindlessly eating in front of the TV or a screen.

Eating together

A huge portion of meals are consumed alone due to busy lifestyles and work commitments. This can be work and school lunches or families and friends just eating at different time due to convenience or trying to slot in meals on the run. Social interaction during mealtimes is becoming increasingly infrequent.

I've read many studies and books discussing that communal eating significantly boosts happiness and life satisfaction. There is a strong correlation between social dining and enhanced well-being, increased social bonds, and a deeper sense of community connection. Social eating plays a critical role in forming and strengthening social networks, which are vital for combating mental and physical health issues and fosters both community cohesion and individual well-being.

Family meals offer a daily opportunity for bonding and communication. They create an environment for open dialogue, laughter, and shared experiences, this fosters a sense of belonging, especially in children and teenagers who are in a critical stage of social development. For couples, preparing and cooking shared meals are an opportunity for focused communication, enhancing their mutual understanding and sharing. Similarly, colleagues benefit from eating together as it provides a relaxed setting for socialising beyond work-related discussions contributing to team buildings.

Family meals also serve as an ideal setting for teaching children healthy eating habits and social skills. Parents act as role models, encouraging the exploration of new foods and teaching the importance of mindful eating and etiquette. This modelling effect extends to dining with friends, where people are more inclined to try new dishes in a social setting.

Sharing plates

Eating as a group significantly broadens the variety of foods available to individuals, which is a cornerstone for good health. In a shared plate setting, meals are typically prepared by different individuals or are catered to a diverse group, comprising various dietary traditions and preferences. This variety ensures that participants are exposed to a broader spectrum of nutrients than they might encounter in their regular, individualised meals.

A communal everyday family meal might include dishes rich in pulses, whole grains, a variety of vegetables, lean proteins, and healthy fats, each contributing unique and essential nutrients. This exposure not only enhances the nutritional value of each meal but also introduces participants to new foods and preparation methods, which can be particularly beneficial to members of the group who haven't tried these foods before. When individuals are exposed to foods that are different from their usual diet but observed as enjoyable and acceptable by their peers, they are more likely to incorporate these new foods into their own diets. This can lead to a more balanced intake of micronutrients and macronutrients, essential for overall health.

Eating in a group setting naturally facilitates portion control, which is crucial for maintaining a healthy weight and preventing conditions like obesity and its related complications. In communal dining scenarios, meals are often served in pre-defined quantities, designed to meet the nutritional needs without excessive caloric intake. This can subtly enforce appropriate portion sizes, unlike individual eating where it's easy to consume a large amount of food in a very short space of time. Observing others can create an unspoken guideline on what and how much to eat, reducing the likelihood of overindulgence.

Eating with children

Family mealtimes provides a structured routine that is beneficial for children, establishing a consistent mealtime environment that fosters both physical and social development. In community settings such as schools, after-school programs, or family gatherings, children sit down at specific times and are often required to wait until everyone is served before eating. This structure not only instils discipline and respect for others but also enhances their social skills by teaching patience and communal participation.

The social nature of community dining also encourages children to experiment with foods they might otherwise avoid. When children observe their peers or adults enjoying different dishes, they become more curious and open to trying them. For example, a child who is reluctant to eat vegetables at home might be more willing to try them after seeing friends eat and enjoy these foods in a school or a community picnic. This peer influence can be incredibly powerful, breaking down a child's resistance to certain foods and broadening their dietary palette, which is crucial for receiving a balanced intake of nutrients.

Family meals play a crucial role in promoting interpersonal communication across various age groups and social backgrounds. These gatherings are not just about eating; they serve as a platform for dialogue, allowing family members to share their experiences, discuss their day, and address any issues they may be facing. This regular interaction strengthens familial bonds and fosters a supportive environment where each member can express themselves openly.

The conversational aspect of family meals is particularly important for children, as it teaches them how to listen, articulate their thoughts, and engage in respectful dialogue. These skills are essential for their social development and are applicable in many other areas of life, including education and future professional environments. Family meals allow children to learn from adults and older siblings, gaining insights and perspectives that contribute to their understanding of the world. This exposure is invaluable in teaching children the importance of conversation and adaptability.

Structuring your mealtimes

To make communal eating a part of your routine, start by setting specific times for meals. This could be breakfast, lunch, or dinner, depending on your lifestyle and commitments. Consider your daily schedule and identify a time when you can consistently sit down for a meal without interruptions. Once you select a time, treat it with the same importance as any other appointment. Enter these mealtimes into your calendar as recurring events and make a conscious effort to keep these slots free from other engagements. This not only establishes a routine but also signals to others that this time is reserved for reconnecting over food. People who work night and evening shifts should also try to eat their main meal at this time, both for the benefits of consuming dinner with the family but also this maintained structure will help you get back to normal eating and sleeping times when you revert back to day shift patterns.

Be open to inviting people outside the family or friend group to dinner. This network could include people from different parts of your life such as work, your area, or your social circles. Aim to share at least one meal per week with this group. You should schedule these occasions well in advance. This not only makes meal planning simpler but also adds variety to the dining experience.

To enrich the experience of shared or family meals, involve your household or guests in the planning and preparation of meals. This could mean assigning tasks based on age and ability, from peeling vegetables to setting the table. For children, this is a great way to teach them about nutrition and cooking, skills that will benefit them for life. For meals involving guests, you might learn what foods and dishes holds significance for them, adding a diversity to the shared meal and engaging conversation.

A dedicated dining space is key to making the most of shared meals. Ensure that your dining area is free from digital distractions such as televisions, phones, and other gadgets. This helps everyone present to fully engage with one another and truly appreciate the food. These spaces provide an opportunity to explore new cuisines and discuss different cultures, thereby broadening your culinary knowledge and understanding food. They also provide a safe space to engage in meaningful conversations.

The science of eating together

During shared meals, there can be an unconscious mimicry of behaviours, such as eating pace and manners. This mirroring
can lead to increased feelings of empathy and understanding. Psychological studies suggest that mimicry and mirroring behaviours during social interactions enhance emotional connections between individuals, making them feel more aligned and in sync with each other.
From a psychological standpoint, eating is fundamentally a pleasurable activity due to the release of neurotransmitters

such as dopamine and serotonin, which are associated with feelings of pleasure and satisfaction like the first bite of a burger or a dessert. When these positive sensations are experienced in a group setting, the brain starts to associate these feel-good neurotransmitters not just with the food, but with the company and the environment. This is known as associative learning.

From an evolutionary biology perspective, the act of eating together has roots in cooperative behaviour, which has been a key factor in human survival. Early humans who shared resources, including food, were more likely to survive and reproduce. This cooperative behaviour extends to modern social interactions, where sharing a meal is often seen as an act of hospitality and goodwill. Such actions reinforce social bonds and the mutual trust necessary for cohesive group functioning.

Chapter Summary & Key Points

- Most meals are consumed in a rush due to busy lifestyles, despite the benefits of slow, mindful eating.

- Mindful eating improves digestion, aids weight management, and enhances meal satisfaction by allowing the body to recognise fullness cues.

- Eating together boosts happiness, social bonds, and life satisfaction, fostering a sense of community and combating mental health issues.

- Communal meals offer diverse nutritional benefits and portion control, exposing individuals to a variety of foods and healthier eating habits.

- Family meals promote children's social development, healthy eating habits, and interpersonal communication through shared experiences and structured routines.

- Learn to cook. Eat less processed food, eat more veg, with family and friends and take your time.

CHAPTER 19
POLYPHENOLS

As mentioned previously in this book, polyphenols are naturally occurring compounds crucial for both plant health and human nutrition. Predominantly found in fruits, vegetables, whole grains, nuts, seeds, and beverages like tea, coffee, and wine, polyphenols enhance the vivid colours and flavours of these foods and offer significant health benefits. These compounds are very important to a plant's defence mechanism against environmental stresses such as the sun, extreme temperatures, drought, and pathogens. This protective function allows plants to endure adverse conditions and plays a role in attracting pollinators through the bright colours of flowers and fruits, which are often due to flavonoids, a type of polyphenol.

The production of polyphenols in response to environmental challenges not only results in distinct colours but also alters the flavour profiles of plants, adding bitter or astringent tastes that contribute to the sensory qualities of foods like the astringency of wine due to grape tannins. These characteristics indicate the presence of beneficial health substances. Polyphenols are classified into several categories, including flavonoids, phenolic acids, lignans, and stilbenes, found in various plant sources. For instance, flavonoids are abundant in fruits, vegetables, tea, and wine, whereas lignans are primarily in seeds and whole grains.

Consuming a range of polyphenol-rich foods and beverages not only supports overall health but also provides an enjoyable dietary experience.

Chronic Disease Prevention

These compounds have been shown to reduce inflammation, lower blood pressure, and improve the health of blood vessels, all of which are important for preventing heart disease. Their antioxidant properties also help in reducing the risk of atherosclerosis, a condition characterised by the hardening and narrowing of the arteries.

Polyphenols can help prevent and manage type 2 diabetes by affecting how the body processes sugar and uses insulin. They help control blood sugar levels by influencing how carbohydrates are digested and absorbed. Polyphenols also have antioxidant and anti-inflammatory effects that protect the brain. They may delay the start and slow the progress of diseases like Alzheimer's and Parkinson's by protecting brain cells and improving brain function.

Polyphenols and the Gut

Polyphenols are broken down by gut bacteria, turning them into forms that the body can absorb more easily, increasing their health benefits. This process also helps the growth of good gut bacteria like Lactobacillus and Bifidobacterium. These beneficial microbes strengthen the gut lining, produce essential vitamins, and support the immune system.

A healthy gut, supported by polyphenols, improves the gut barrier, preventing harmful substances from entering the bloodstream and lowering the risk of inflammation and related diseases. Polyphenols and their by-products can also influence the immune system by promoting anti-inflammatory compounds and reducing those that cause inflammation, thus lowering the risk of chronic diseases.

By boosting the growth of good gut bacteria, polyphenols help keep a healthy balance in the gut, preventing harmful bacteria from taking over and reducing the risk of infections and gut-related issues.

Polyphenol-Rich Nutrition

Incorporating polyphenols into your diet is not only beneficial for health but can also be delicious and enjoyable. Focus on consuming fruits and vegetables that are in season and sourced locally. Seasonal produce is likely to be fresher and contain higher levels of polyphenols due to reduced transportation and storage time. Local farmers' markets are excellent sources for such items, which also helps support the local economy.

Integrate a variety of herbs and spices into your meals. Spices such as paprika, cumin, cloves, star anise, and cinnamon, and herbs like basil, peppermint, oregano, and sage are not only flavourful but are also high in polyphenols. These can be added to recipes at the during the cooking process, teas, marinades, or even sprinkled over salads and cooked dishes.

Look at plant-based proteins such as legumes and tofu, which are good sources of polyphenols. For instance, soybeans and lentils not only provide protein but also contribute polyphenols, adding to the diversity of these compounds in your diet.

Swapping typical snack foods like crisps and milk chocolate for raw nuts, seeds, and dark chocolate with over 70% cocoa can give you a quick polyphenol boost. These snacks are easy to fit into a busy lifestyle and offer many health benefits.

Dark chocolate with at least 70% cocoa is essential because anything less than this amount won't provide the health benefits associated with polyphenols. The higher cocoa content ensures a richer source of polyphenols, which are powerful antioxidants. These antioxidants help reduce inflammation, improve heart health, and support brain function. Lower cocoa content in chocolate means more added sugars and fats, diluting the beneficial effects of polyphenols.

Experiment with different cooking methods to maximize polyphenol intake. For instance, steaming or microwaving vegetables instead of boiling can help preserve the polyphenol content. Use cooking water from vegetables like spinach or broccoli in soups or sauces to ensure you're getting all the possible nutrients.

Plan your meals around fruits and vegetables first. This could mean adding berries to your breakfast yogurt, having a side salad rich in mixed greens and colourful vegetables with lunch, and including a vegetable stir-fry with dinner.

While it's mentioned to enjoy beverages like green tea and coffee in moderation, expanding your range to include herbal teas such as hibiscus or matcha which can further boost your polyphenol intake. These beverages can be a relaxing, low-calorie way to increase polyphenols.

The rule of 30

Remember the rule of trying to eat at least 30 different plant varieties into your diet each week, the task can seem daunting. However, spices and herbs are some of the most polyphenol-rich foods available, and they offer a simple way to diversify the plants in your diet.

Experiment with different combinations of herbs and spices. For example, combine oregano and thyme in Mediterranean dishes, or mix coriander and lime zest for a fresh, zesty taste. Each combination can transform the same base ingredients into a completely different dish, helping to keep your meals interesting and varied.

Create your own dry rubs and seasoning mixes using a variety of ground spices and dried herbs. This not only ensures you are cooking with ingredients free of additives but also makes it easier to apply a diverse range of polyphenols to simple dishes like grilled meats and vegetables. Most air fryers have a dehydrate function so take you vegetable trimmings and bits of vegetables that are a little past their best in the fridge and dehydrate them until crisps, smash these into powders in your food processors then use this to season meats, fish and vegetables as an easy way to get more polyphenols but also use up vegetables that would be wasted otherwise. By thinking this way and putting fruits and vegetable first at every meal, consuming 30 different plants a week is very achievable, with a small amount of planning you could probably get 30 varieties of plants into a single meal!

Chapter Summary & Key Points

- Polyphenols are naturally occurring compounds found in plants, contributing to their colour, flavour, and defence against environmental stresses.

- Polyphenols play a critical role in preventing chronic diseases by modulating inflammation, supporting heart health, improving glucose metabolism, and offering neuroprotective properties.

- In the gut, polyphenols are metabolised by bacteria, improving the absorption and efficacy of these compounds. They promote the growth of beneficial gut bacteria, enhance gut barrier integrity, and modulate the immune response to reduce inflammation.

- Don't overcook your vegetables, light steaming, roasting or stir frying retains the nutrients.

- Try to eat 30 different plant varieties each week to get the benefits of a diverse variety of polyphenols. This includes herbs and spices, so the better you make your food taste, the better it is for you.

- Learn to cook. Eat less processed food and eat more vegetables, plants are the source of all polyphenols.

CHAPTER 20
SAVVY SHOPPING AND CHOOSING YOUR FOODS

A well-planned supermarket trip is crucial for maintaining a balanced diet and ensuring that you have everything you need for the week ahead. The process begins with planning your main meals. By deciding in advance what you will eat for breakfast, lunch, and dinner each day, you can create a detailed shopping list that includes all necessary ingredients. This approach helps avoid impulse purchases and ensures that you only buy what you need.

Including planned takeaways and meals out in your schedule is equally important. Knowing when you will be eating out allows you to adjust your shopping list, accordingly, preventing you from over-purchasing perishable items that might go to waste. For instance, if you plan to dine out on Friday evening, you won't need to buy ingredients for dinner on that day. This sounds like a given but factor in times you may or may not eat out also. Chances are if you scheduled to be out you need to factor in either eating out or shopping for snacks or a packed meal to bring with you. The packed meal option will most likely be the healthiest as you have full control as to how it is prepared.

Planning for snacks is also essential. By choosing healthy snacks ahead of time, such as fruits, nuts, or yogurt, you can avoid reaching for unhealthy options when you get caught out and hungry. Including these in your shopping list ensures you have good quality snacks readily available, without reaching for ultra-processed convenience foods.

Stocktake before you shop

Before heading to the supermarket, it's a good idea to take stock of what you already have at home. This practice helps you avoid overbuying and ensures that no food goes to waste. Begin by checking your pantry, refrigerator, and freezer to see what ingredients you already have. Make a list of these items and plan your meals around them, prioritising perishable goods that need to be used soon.

When it comes to fresh produce, if you have vegetables or fruits that are nearing their use by date, consider how you can use them in the next day or two. For example, vegetables can be incorporated into stir-fries, salads, or soups and should be chopped up to prepare to make these at this point, so they are ready to use first. If you find that you have more fresh produce than you can use immediately, a great strategy is to batch cook and freeze meals. Batch cooking involves preparing large quantities of food at once and then freezing it in portions for later use. For instance, you can make a big pot of curry or a hearty pasta sauce using your fresh vegetables and a tin of tomatoes with some tomato puree. Once cooked, let the food cool, then portion it into zip-lock bags or airtight containers. Label each bag with the contents and the date it was made, then store them in the freezer. This way, you create your own ready meals, which can be quickly reheated during the week when you're short on time.

By taking stock and planning your meals around what you already have, you can significantly reduce food waste and avoid unnecessary purchases. Batch cooking not only saves time during busy weekdays but also makes your shopping more efficient and economical. This approach ensures you always have nutritious, home-cooked meals ready to go, helping you avoid the trap of ultra-processed convenience foods or ready meals.

Read the labels

I go into this in a later chapter in more detail, but reading labels during a supermarket shopping trip is essential for making informed choices about the foods you purchase and consume. While the traffic light system on food packaging can provide a quick visual cue about the levels of fat, saturated fat, sugar, and salt, it is not always a reliable indicator of nutritional quality. Some ultra-processed foods might have low levels of these nutrients, so they will show up as green on the label, yet still be unhealthy due to the presence of artificial sweeteners, thickeners, and emulsifiers. These additives can affect the body's metabolism and overall health, even if the product appears healthy at first glance.

When examining food labels, the list of ingredients is often more telling than the calorie count. Calories provide a measure of energy but do not indicate the nutritional value or quality of the food. For instance, a low-calorie product could still be filled with artificial additives and lack essential nutrients. Therefore, prioritising the ingredient list over calorie content is crucial. Ideally, the ingredients should be whole foods that you recognise, such as vegetables, grains, and lean proteins. If a product contains a long list of chemicals or unfamiliar terms, it is best to avoid it, as it likely indicates high levels of processing and artificial additives.

Another critical aspect of reading labels is understanding portion sizes. Nutritional information is often given per 100 grams, but the actual portion you consume might be much larger. For example, if a ready meal shows it contains 5 grams of sugar per 100 grams, but the entire meal weighs 400 grams, you would actually be consuming 20 grams of sugar, which is equivalent to four teaspoons. The same logic applies to salt and fat content. This discrepancy can lead to unintentionally consuming more unhealthy ingredients than intended.

Shop the perimeter

Shopping in the perimeter aisles of the supermarket (the aisle all around the outer walls) offers several advantages for maintaining a healthy diet as its usually the outer perimeter isles of a supermarket where the whole foods are kept. In most supermarkets the first isle on the perimeter is the fresh fruits and vegetables. These are essential components of a balanced diet, providing vital vitamins, minerals, and fibre. In addition to fresh produce, the perimeter aisles typically house fresh meat, poultry, fish, and dairy products. By shopping along the perimeter, you are more likely to choose whole, minimally processed foods that contribute to a well-rounded diet. These whole foods found in the perimeter aisles are beneficial because they often contain fewer additives and preservatives compared to processed foods. These minimally processed items are generally more nutrient-dense, meaning they provide more vitamins and minerals per calorie.

Another advantage of shopping the perimeter aisles is that the foods available often change with the seasons. Seasonal produce not only tastes better and is more affordable, but it also ensures a variety of flavours and nutrients throughout the year. Eating seasonally can make meals more interesting and ensuring a diversity of ingredients and foods you eat, meaning a diverse intake of nutrients.

In contrast, the centre aisles of supermarkets are typically filled with processed foods that may be high in sugar, salt, and unhealthy fats, and often contain numerous additives and preservatives. These foods can be less nutritious and more calorie-dense, contributing to poor health outcomes when consumed in excess.

Fresh fruits & vegetables aisle

You should prioritise choosing a variety of fresh fruits and vegetables and use these as the base for all your meals and snacks. A diverse selection of produce ensures that you get a broad spectrum of vitamins, minerals, and antioxidants, which are vital for maintaining good health and preventing chronic diseases. Filling up your fruit bowl with different types of fruits provides easy access to healthy snacks, making it more likely that you will reach for a good food decision rather than an unhealthy snack.

In addition to selecting a wide range of fruits and vegetables, it is important to shop for flavouring plants such as fresh herbs, garlic, chilli, and ginger. These ingredients not only enhance the taste of your dishes but also add significant nutritional benefits. Fresh herbs like basil, parsley, and coriander are rich in antioxidants and essential vitamins. Garlic, chilli, and ginger have potent anti-inflammatory and immune-boosting properties, on top of this they will make your dishes more flavourful and exciting to eat.

Many supermarkets offer weekly promotions on various vegetables and fruits, which can be a great opportunity to experiment with new ingredients. Introducing unfamiliar produce into your diet can bring new flavours and textures to your meals, making eating more enjoyable. Different fruits and vegetables have unique nutritional profiles, so trying new ones can provide your body with a broader array of nutrients.

Meat and Poultry aisle

When selecting beef, lamb, and pork, it's important to be mindful of their saturated fat content. These meats often have marbling, which refers to the streaks of fat dispersed throughout the meat. While marbling can enhance flavour and tenderness, it also means these meats are higher in saturated fats, which should be consumed in moderation to maintain heart health.

Processed deli meats, such as pre-packaged ham slices, should be avoided where possible. These products are often loaded with nitrates and preservatives, which have been linked to various health issues, including an increased risk of cancer. Additionally, processed meats tend to be higher in sodium and other additives. A more nutritious and economical alternative is to buy a whole joint of meat like a ham joint, cook it yourself, and slice it as needed. This method not only reduces your intake of harmful preservatives but also allows you to control the quality and quantity of meat consumed.

Chicken and turkey are excellent choices for lean meats because most of their saturated fat content is found in the skin. By removing the skin, you significantly reduce the fat intake, making these options healthier. These poultry choices are also versatile and can be used in a variety of dishes, providing high-quality protein with less fat.

Meat on the bone, such as chicken thighs or beef short ribs, often contains a bit more saturated fat compared to boneless cuts. However, these cuts also offer additional nutritional benefits. The bones and cartilage are rich in nutrients like collagen, which can support joint health and skin elasticity. Cooking meat on the bone can also enhance the flavour value of your dishes especially when they are braised with lots of vegetables and consumed in moderation.

When selecting minced meat, always be aware of the fat content. Minced meat can vary significantly in its fat percentage, so opting for leaner versions under 8-10% fat at a minimum. When buying any meat choose unseasoned and unmarinated meats to avoid added sugars, salts, and preservatives. By seasoning or marinating meat at home, you have full control over the ingredients, ensuring a healthier meal.

Dairy aisle

Shopping in the dairy aisle requires thoughtful choices to ensure you're selecting the most nutritious options. One of the key considerations I personally choose is full-fat milk over low-fat varieties. Full-fat milk is more nutrient-dense because it retains fat-soluble nutrients such as vitamins A, D, E, and K, which are partially removed when the fat is skimmed off. Additionally, full-fat milk contains only about 3.5% fat, making it a less processed choice.

When comparing dairy milk to plant-based alternatives like oat and almond milk, it's important to note that plant milks are essentially water blended with oats or almonds and then strained. While these alternatives can be suitable for those with specific dietary restrictions, full-fat cow's milk is generally far more nutritious, offering a well-rounded profile of essential nutrients.

In the cheese section, choosing high-quality natural cheeses is preferable to processed cheese slices. Quality cheeses are rich in flavour and nutrients, while processed cheese products often contain additives, preservatives, and artificial ingredients that diminish their nutritional value.

Non-flavoured live yoghurt is the best choice as it contains natural fats and beneficial probiotics without added sugars. Many yoghurts marketed as "gut friendly", "no added sugar" and "low fat" often contain hidden sugars from fruit sources and have added thickeners and stabilisers to mimic the creaminess of full-fat yoghurt, making them ultra-processed foods. A small pot of flavoured yoghurt can contain as much as four teaspoons of sugar per serving, which can be detrimental to health when consumed regularly. These are often marketed at children.

When it comes to spreads, real butter is my preferred choice compared to "healthy" spreadable dairy products. Butter contains only one ingredient—milk—whereas spreads often have a long list of chemicals to achieve the right texture and colour. These additives can detract from the nutritional quality of the product.

I must note in this section that heart disease remains one of the leading causes of death in Ireland, making dietary choices particularly crucial in managing and mitigating risk. Saturated fats, found in full-fat dairy products, have been linked to increased cholesterol levels, a significant risk factor for heart disease. Although full-fat dairy products contain essential fat-soluble vitamins such as A, D, E, and K, their high saturated fat content means they should be consumed in moderation. Excessive consumption of saturated fats can lead to the build-up of LDL cholesterol (often referred to as "bad" cholesterol) in the arteries. This build-up can form plaques, leading to atherosclerosis, which restricts blood flow and can result in heart attacks or strokes. Given the prevalence of heart disease, it is vital to balance the intake of full-fat dairy with other low-fat or fat-free alternatives to maintain cardiovascular health.

While full-fat dairy products offer nutritional benefits, it is essential to integrate them sparingly within a balanced diet. Incorporating a variety of fat sources, such as unsaturated fats from fish, nuts, seeds, and olive oil, can help maintain a healthy lipid profile. Should you be advised to reduce your saturated fat intake, I would suggest drizzling bread with olive oil before grilling or spreading avocados on your toast as a far better option than a dairy spread reformulated to reduce the saturated fat.

Lastly, when buying eggs, always choose free-range eggs where possible. The quality of free-range eggs is generally higher, with richer yolks and better flavour. If you can find a local supplier with free-range chickens, you'll likely notice a remarkable difference in the quality compared to supermarket eggs.

Dry Goods Aisle

When shopping in the pantry staples aisle, making thoughtful choices can significantly enhance the nutritional quality of your meals. For those who enjoy baking, experimenting with wholemeal flour in recipes is a great idea. Wholemeal flour retains the bran and germ of the grain, providing more fibre, vitamins, and minerals than refined white flour. This switch can improve the nutritional profile of your baked goods and these flours add more of a nutty flavour profile to your baked goods.

Sugar, while often demonised, is a natural food product that our bodies are designed to break down. Consumed in moderation, there is no need to replace it with artificial sweeteners or fancy alternatives marketed for health reasons. Our bodies process agave syrup, honey, and maple syrup in much the same way as table sugar. However, if you prefer the flavour or convenience of these pourable sugars, they are perfectly fine to use just be aware they can be expensive and don't hold any great nutritional benefit over sugar.

Tinned goods are pantry essentials that can be both convenient and nutritious. Items like chickpeas, lentils, and kidney beans are fantastic choices, offering plant-based protein, fibre, and various nutrients. However, be cautious with canned goods in sauces, such as baked beans, as they can be high in added sugars and preservatives. Choosing plain canned beans and adding your own seasoning is often a healthier choice.

Jarred sauces can be convenient but are typically expensive and contain many additives and preservatives. Making your sauces at home allows you to control the ingredients and avoid unnecessary additives. However, some jarred spice pastes (like a Thai curry paste) can be a valuable addition to your cooking, providing a convenient way to add complex flavours to your dishes. Just ensure they contain minimal preservatives.

Condiments, while sometimes high in artificial flavours and preservatives, are usually consumed in small quantities, making their impact less significant. Using condiments like Sriracha sauce (which may have thickeners and preservatives in it) on stir-fried vegetables or Ketchup (which may have added sugars and flavourings) can enhance the flavour without overwhelming the nutritional benefits of the meal.

A well-stocked spice rack is essential for any kitchen. Spices not only add flavour to your meals but also provide various health benefits due to their plant-based compounds. Including a variety of spices in your cooking can make your meals more exciting and nutritionally rich.

When it comes to grains and pasta, making informed choices can greatly enhance the nutritional quality of your meals. Opting for brown rice over white rice is a simple yet effective switch, as brown rice contains more fibre, vitamins, and minerals. The fibre in brown rice aids digestion, helps maintain stable blood sugar levels, and contributes to a feeling of fullness. However, it is even more beneficial to explore a variety of other grains such as quinoa, barley, and buckwheat. These grains offer different textures and flavours while providing a diverse range of nutrients. Additionally, finely chopped vegetables stir-fried as a rice alternative, like cauliflower rice, can be a creative and nutritious option, adding more fibre and vitamins to your meals.

For pasta, while brown pasta is generally a healthier choice compared to white pasta due to its higher fibre content, there are other exciting options to consider. Fresh egg-based pasta offers a rich flavour and satisfying texture. If you are feeling adventurous, you might try making pasta at home using 00 flour, which is finely ground and perfect for pasta-making. The basic recipe is simple: one egg per 100 grams of 00 flour. Mix the ingredients into a dough, roll it out thinly, and slice it into ribbons with a knife. Homemade pasta can be a rewarding and delicious addition to your meals and great fun to make with children which I do with my kids regularly.

Among all starches, potatoes and sweet potatoes stand out as particularly nutritious options. They provide essential vitamins and minerals, such as vitamin C, potassium, and beta-carotene in sweet potatoes. However, it is important to ensure that these starchy vegetables, rice or pasta occupy less than a quarter of your plate at mealtimes. This allows for a balanced meal that includes a variety of other food groups, ensuring you get a broad range of nutrients.

Oils and fats

When selecting oils and fats, extra virgin olive oil should be your top priority due to its numerous health benefits. Rich in monounsaturated fats and antioxidants, extra virgin olive oil has been linked to reduced inflammation, improved heart health, and protection against chronic diseases. However, it is important to note that extra virgin olive oil degrades at high temperatures, making it less suitable for high-heat cooking. To ensure the best quality, check the label for a single country of origin, which indicates that the oil is not a blend of different oils, thus maintaining its purity and beneficial properties.

For cooking at higher temperatures, coconut oil and rapeseed oil are better options. These oils can withstand higher heat without degrading, making them suitable for frying and sautéing. However, they should be used in moderation. Coconut oil, while stable at high temperatures, is high in saturated fats, which should be consumed in limited amounts. Rapeseed oil, also known as canola oil, is a good source of omega-3 fatty acids but should be balanced with other healthy fats in your diet like extra virgin olive oil.

Vegetable oil and sunflower oil, although often the cheapest options, have inflammatory properties and should generally be avoided. These oils are high in omega-6 fatty acids, which can promote inflammation when consumed in excess. If you purchase these oils for deep-fat frying, it is worth considering Alternative cooking methods. Using an air fryer or oven roasting can achieve similar results with significantly less oil, reducing the potential health risks associated with consuming large amounts of inflammatory fats.

Snacks aisle

When shopping for snacks, it is important to make choices that provide nutritional value rather than just empty calories. Most crisps, for example, are essentially just starches and oils of varying qualities, offering little in the way of nutrient density. They are often high in unhealthy fats and sodium, making them a less desirable option for regular consumption.

Crackers and rice cakes, while not particularly nutrient-dense, can serve as useful vehicles for more nutritious toppings, especially for children. Topping these with nut butters, fruits, or cheeses can help provide children with the calories and nutrients they might be reluctant to consume otherwise. These combinations can make snacks more appealing and nutritious, offering essential proteins, fats, and vitamins.

The optimal snacks in the snack's aisle are nuts. Nuts are rich in healthy fats, protein, fibre, vitamins, and minerals. Consuming a packet containing different varieties like cashews, hazelnuts, and pecan etc rather than just a packet of peanuts is beneficial because different nuts offer different nutrients. For example, almonds are high in vitamin E and magnesium, while walnuts are an excellent source of omega-3 fatty acids. A good variety ensures a more balanced intake of essential nutrients.

Popcorn without flavourings is another excellent snack option. It is high in fibre and low in calories, making it a filling and satisfying snack. Popcorn can help you feel full for longer periods, reducing the likelihood of overeating.

It's also important to consider the calorie content and nutritional quality of snacks. For example, a packet of highly processed corn snacks might have only 90 calories, whereas a bag of nuts might have 250 calories. However, the body excretes about a third of the calories from nuts because they are hard to break down. Additionally, you will burn more calories digesting nuts due to their tough and hard to digest structure. As a result, consuming nuts may provide you with similar or more digestible calories than processed corn snacks, but with far greater nutritional benefits. Nuts also help boost your metabolism because they are more challenging to digest which means you will burn more calories and increase your metabolic rate by digesting them.

Cereal and Breakfast Foods

When shopping for cereal and breakfast foods, it is essential to be aware of their nutritional content. Many cereals, particularly those marketed to children, are extremely high in sugar. By reading the label, you can determine the amount of sugar per portion, often revealing that a serving contains several teaspoons of sugar. However, it's important to note that the average portion size consumed is typically twice what is suggested on the box, meaning that the actual sugar intake can be quite substantial in one sitting. This is particularly concerning for children, who may consume much more sugar than recommended or that their parents think from reading a misleading label.

A healthier alternative is opting for oats, which can be prepared as porridge or used for overnight oats. These dishes are versatile and can serve as a vehicle for a variety of additions such as berries, chia seeds, flaxseeds, and fresh fruits. This not only enhances the flavour but also significantly boosts the nutritional value, providing fibre, vitamins, and antioxidants.

Muesli is another popular breakfast option, but many commercial varieties are high in sugar. It is far more beneficial to make your own low-sugar version at home. Homemade muesli can be stored for a long time and allows you to control the ingredients. You can include a mix of rolled oats, nuts, seeds, and dried fruits without adding sugars as dried fruit already has a high sugar content.

Breakfast bars are often perceived as a convenient option, but they generally have a nutritional profile like confectionary bars. Many are high in sugar and contain various additives, making them unsuitable as a healthy breakfast choice. It's important to consider these products in the same category as sweets and not rely on them for a heathy breakfast alternative for adults or children.

Chocolate, sweets, and biscuits

When shopping for chocolate, sweets, and biscuits, it is important to approach these items as indulgences and select the highest quality to maximise enjoyment and not worry too much about the nutritional benefits. However, high-quality chocolate, particularly varieties with over 70% cocoa solids, offers several health benefits. Dark chocolate is rich in antioxidants, particularly flavonoids, which have been linked to improved heart health, reduced inflammation, and enhanced brain function. It also contains minerals such as iron, magnesium, and zinc. By choosing chocolate with a higher cocoa content, you can enjoy these benefits while consuming less sugar and fewer additives compared to milk chocolate.

Recognising that chocolate, sweets, and biscuits are treats, it is worthwhile to select the best quality indulgences you can afford. High-quality products are often more satisfying, allowing you to appreciate the indulgence more fully. For example, biscuits and cookies that are mass-produced and cost only one euro per packet typically uses cheap, processed ingredients at every stage of production. These products often contain artificial flavours, preservatives, and hydrogenated fats, which will negatively impact your health. In contrast, biscuits made with real butter and high-quality ingredients from reputable makers are more likely to deliver a better flavour and texture. This principle extends to all indulgences, including baked goods and doughnuts. Choosing treats made with natural, high-quality ingredients not only enhances the taste experience but can also mean fewer artificial additives and healthier fats.

When selecting indulgences, consider looking for quality products that prioritise quality ingredients. These items may be more expensive, but their superior taste and potential nutritional benefits can justify the cost. For baked goods, opting for items made with real butter, whole grains, and natural sweeteners can provide a more memorable indulgence than a mass-produced product. For an even better product learn how to bake them yourself at home, your baked products will not be any healthier, but they will taste great, you have full control of the ingredients and children love to get involved.

Frozen Foods aisle

Shopping in the frozen food aisle offers both advantages and considerations for maintaining a healthy diet. One of the key benefits of frozen vegetables and fruits is that they are often more nutrient-packed than their fresh counterparts. This is because they are frozen at their peak ripeness, capturing the nutrients at that point in time. However, while frozen vegetables and fruits retain their nutritional value, they may lack the crunch and texture of fresh produce, which can impact their taste and culinary appeal.

Fresh vegetables and fruits generally offer a more satisfying texture and flavour, making them preferable for certain dishes, although frozen options like peas and frozen berries have a place in all kitchens.

Frozen ready meals and pizzas, while convenient, often fall short in comparison to freshly made products. These pre-packaged meals can be more expensive than preparing similar dishes at home and usually contain higher levels of sodium, preservatives, and unhealthy fats. Although they provide a quick solution for busy times, they cannot match the nutritional quality or taste of homemade meals.

The consumption of frozen chicken nuggets and fish fingers is particularly high among children. However, these products are often highly processed and lack the nutritional value of fresh chicken or fish. Homemade versions, where fresh chicken or fish is coated and baked, are far healthier options. These homemade alternatives allow you to control the ingredients and avoid the excessive sodium and additives commonly found in frozen varieties.

When it comes to ice cream and desserts, it is important to treat these items as indulgences. They should be consumed sparingly and in moderation. Choose smaller portions of higher quality ice-creams and desserts made with high-quality ingredients. There are lots of artisan Irish brands making ice cream with very high-quality ingredients. This is preferable to mass-produced industrial products. High-quality desserts tend to be more satisfying and flavourful, making them a better choice when you decide to indulge.

Shopping for Beverages

When shopping for beverages, try to consider their impact on your health. All soft drinks, whether regular or diet, should be avoided as part of a healthy diet. Regular soft drinks are high in sugar, providing empty calories that offer no nutritional value and can lead to weight gain and other health issues. Diet soft drinks, on the other hand, contain artificial sweeteners and chemicals that can disrupt your gut bacteria. Additionally, these drinks can increase your cravings for sweetness, leading to a higher intake of sweet and starchy foods later in the day. This is due to an insulin response from the quick delivery of sugar to your system.

As boring as it sounds water is the preferred beverage for maintaining good health. It is essential for hydration and overall bodily functions. While bottled water often claims various health benefits, it offers no significant advantage over tap water. Therefore, if you choose to buy water, sparkling water makes the most sense (providing you like the taste) as it provides a different drinking experience that you can't easily replicate at home.

Fruit juices, although derived from fresh fruit, are essentially just sugar in the form of fructose and water. The juicing process removes the fibre and releases the sugars from the fruit's cells, making these drinks like sugary soft drinks in their effect on the body. Without the fibre and structure of the whole fruit to slow absorption, the sugar in fruit juice can cause rapid spikes in blood sugar levels.

Smoothies, while often seen as a healthy option, come with certain considerations. The blitzing process breaks down the cell walls of the fruit, releasing sugars that were previously enclosed within the fibre. These released sugars, known as "free sugars," are more readily absorbed by the body. This rapid absorption can lead to spikes in blood sugar levels, similar to the effect of consuming sugary soft drinks.

When it comes to alcoholic beverages, it's important to understand that all forms of alcohol are essentially a poison. If you choose to drink alcohol, it should be viewed as an indulgence that can disrupt your sleep and lead to poor food decisions. Although a glass of red wine is often touted for its potential health benefits due to its antioxidant content, alcohol in any form disrupts both sleep and your gut bacteria. Think about how we used alcohol-based sanitizers during the Covid-19 pandemic to kill bacteria. The same alcohol in beverages has a similar effect on the beneficial microbes in your gut when you consume it.

Bakery Isle

Shopping in the bakery aisle of a supermarket requires a critical eye, as most of the breads and rolls found here are highly processed. These products often contain numerous emulsifiers, preservatives, and other additives, making them ultra-processed foods. Mass produced bread you find in supermarkets is essentially a baked wheat-based mousse with an artificially extended shelf life, and vastly different from fresh, traditionally baked bread.

In contrast, bread from an artisan sourdough baker is far more beneficial. Artisan sourdough typically contains only three ingredients: salt, water, and flour. This simple ingredient list ensures that the bread is free from unnecessary additives and preservatives. By comparison, I counted 17 ingredients in one particular supermarket loaf, many of which were unrecognisable as base ingredients for bread.

The same issues apply to pastries, cakes, and other baked goods in the supermarket bakery aisle. These items often contain a long list of additives and preservatives to enhance their shelf life and texture, making them far less nutritious than their homemade or artisan counterparts.

Learning to bake bread at home is a highly rewarding practice and a great activity to do with children. It gives you complete control over the ingredients, allowing you to avoid unnecessary additives and incorporate a variety of seeds and flavours to suit your tastes. Homemade bread can be frozen once it has cooled from the oven, providing you with fresh, healthy bread throughout the week. A great starting point for home baking is buttermilk soda bread, which is one of the easiest and quickest types of bread to make.

By baking your own bread or buying from an artisan baker you ensure that your family enjoys proper, additive-free bread. Also, when you bake bread yourself you can experiment with different recipes and ingredients like seeds and herbs to keep things interesting.

Seafood

When shopping for seafood in the supermarket, it's important to consider the freshness and sourcing of the products. Fresh seafood may not always be as fresh as it appears, especially if the supermarket does not have a high turnover of seafood. This can affect the quality and taste of the fish. Therefore, it's crucial to be aware of the supermarket's seafood turnover rate to ensure you are getting the freshest options available.

Frozen seafood, such as prawns, can be a very convenient option. Prawns defrost quickly and can be a lifesaver when you need to prepare a meal in a hurry. They retain their nutritional value well when frozen, making them a practical and nutritious choice for various dishes.

Salmon is the most purchased fish in supermarkets. Most supermarket salmon is farmed, which ensures a consistent supply of fresh fish. Farmed salmon is a good source of oily fish, rich in omega-3 fatty acids, which are essential for heart health. Similarly, farmed trout, especially from reputable Irish trout farms, is also a good option. It arrives at the supermarket fresh and provides similar nutritional benefits as salmon. Smoked salmon is another convenient product that works wonderfully in salads and green vegetable dishes. It offers a rich, smoky flavour and retains many of the nutritional benefits of fresh salmon, making it a versatile and nutritious addition to meals.

Tinned fish, such as mackerel and sardines, are excellent sources of protein and omega-3 fatty acids. However, it's important to be cautious about the sauces or oils they are canned in, as these can add unnecessary fats and sugars. Choose tinned fish in water or olive oil for a healthier choice. Tinned tuna is also a great source of protein and is very versatile in the kitchen. However, it is not an oily fish and does not provide the high levels of omega-3 fatty acids found in salmon, mackerel, and sardines. It's still a valuable addition to your diet but should be complemented with other fish to ensure a balanced intake of omega-3s.

International Foods aisle

The International Foods aisle of the supermarket offers firsthand look at different cuisines from around the world, providing an excellent opportunity to diversify your diet and expand your palate. Trying new foods is not only an enjoyable culinary activity but also brings significant health benefits, particularly when it comes to fermented foods such as sauerkraut from Eastern Europe, miso from Japan, and kimchi from Korea.

Fermented foods like these are rich in live bacteria, which are great for your gut health. Sauerkraut, made from fermented cabbage, is a source of probiotics that can improve digestion and boost the immune system. Miso, a traditional Japanese seasoning made from fermented soybeans, is not only a flavour enhancer but also supports gut health with its probiotic content. Kimchi, a staple in Korean cuisine, is a spicy fermented vegetable dish that provides a wealth of probiotics and vitamins. Incorporating these fermented foods into your diet can help maintain a healthy balance of gut bacteria, which is crucial for digestion, nutrient absorption, and immune function. They also add unique flavours and textures to your meals, making your diet more varied and interesting.

Beyond fermented foods, the International Foods aisle introduces you to a diverse array of plants, pickles, and spices. This diversity is key to a healthy diet, as different foods provide different nutrients, helping to ensure you get a broad spectrum of vitamins, minerals, and other beneficial compounds. For example, Indian spices like turmeric and cumin have anti-inflammatory properties, while Mediterranean olives and olive oil are rich in healthy fats.

Health and Wellness aisle

Shopping in the health section of a supermarket can be a bit overwhelming with the myriad of options available with myriad of health claims.

Organic foods are often considered to be of better quality and more nutrient-dense compared to conventional foods. However, they are typically more expensive. It's important to note that mass-produced organic foods might meet the criteria for organic certification but may not always align fully with the principles of the organic movement, which emphasises sustainability and minimal processing. If you are seriously considering incorporating more organic foods into your diet, it might be more rewarding and cost-effective to grow your own produce. Gardening not only ensures that you have truly organic food but also offers the added benefits of physical activity and exposure to beneficial bacteria in the soil, which can improve your overall health.

Gluten-free products have become very popular, but it's essential to understand that they do not provide any additional health benefits for those who do not have a gluten intolerance or celiac disease. For most people, these products offer no taste advantage either and can sometimes be less nutritious due to the removal of certain grains that are beneficial in a regular diet. Gluten free flour is an excellent flour to use as a crispy coating on meats and vegetables before frying or roasting. This is because the flour itself contains no gluten so it's very brittle and it's this property that adds a crunch when used in this way.

Vegan and vegetarian options are plentiful in the health section, but many of these products can be highly processed, especially those designed to mimic the taste and texture of meat. Highly processed vegetarian and vegan foods may contain additives, preservatives, and other artificial ingredients that diminish their nutritional value. It's generally better to purchase plant-based foods in their whole form from the fruit and vegetable aisle. Whole foods like beans, lentils, vegetables, fruits, nuts, and seeds are naturally nutritious and can be used to create delicious, healthful plant-based meals.

When considering supplements, it's always best to evaluate and improve your diet first. Supplements can be beneficial, especially Vitamin D in the winter, but they should not replace a balanced diet. A diet rich in a variety of plants, nuts and seeds, good quality proteins, and some fermented foods can often provide the nutrients you need. Whole foods contain a complex matrix of nutrients and other beneficial compounds that supplements cannot replicate. Therefore, getting nutrients from your food is always preferable so it's best to look at your diet first and only consider supplements if recommended by a medical professional.

Look outside the supermarket.

Shopping locally with artisan producers instead of in supermarkets offers numerous benefits that significantly impact both the quality of our food and the health of our communities. Craft butchers, vegetable growers, artisan bakers, and small batch food producers are the very essence of Irish cuisine. Their dedication to quality and tradition ensures that we enjoy some of the best produce and products available.

Celebrating and supporting these artisans is essential to preserving the rich culinary heritage of Ireland.

Our modern food system, dominated by large supermarkets, often undermines these small producers. Supermarkets tend to control the entire output of growers and food producers, leading to a highly centralised supply chain. This centralisation restricts the variety of products available to consumers and allows supermarkets to set prices that might not always reflect the true value or cost of production. Consequently, the focus shifts from quality and sustainability to efficiency and profit maximisation. By choosing to shop with local artisans, you are making a conscious decision to support a more sustainable and ethical food system. **Every euro spent at a local butcher, baker, or farmer is a vote for the continuation of high-quality, traditional food production**. This choice helps to ensure that small-scale producers can continue their craft, which often involves methods passed down through generations, resulting in products that are superior in taste and nutritional value.

Knowing the people who produce your food and understanding the care and effort they put into their work creates a greater appreciation for what you eat. It also encourages more responsible and informed food choices. In contrast, the anonymity of the supermarket experience can lead to a disconnect from these values. The convenience and often lower prices of supermarkets can be tempting, but this comes at the cost of supporting practices that may not prioritise quality, sustainability, or fair compensation for producers and growers.

By choosing to support local artisans, you contribute to a healthier, more vibrant, and more diverse food culture. This not only benefits you and your family but also strengthens the community and helps to preserve the unique flavours and traditions of Irish cuisine.

Chapter Summary & Key Points

- Plan your meals ahead, including snacks and dining out, to avoid unnecessary purchases and food waste.

- Take stock of existing pantry and fridge items before shopping to prevent overbuying and to use perishable items first.

- Batch cook and freeze meals before you shop to use up what's there, save time and reduce waste, ensuring you have healthy options available.

- Read food labels, focusing on the ingredient list rather than calorie count, and avoid products with artificial additives.

- Shop the perimeter aisles for fresh, minimally processed foods, and prioritize seasonal produce for better taste and affordability.

- Choose a variety of fresh fruits and vegetables for diverse nutrients and use fresh herbs and spices to enhance flavour and health benefits.

- Select lean meats, avoid processed deli meats, and consider the nutritional benefits of meat on the bone and homemade versions.

- In the dairy aisle, go for good quality milk and cheese, and processed dairy products. Choose non-flavoured live yoghurt.

- Choose wholemeal flour for baking and plain canned goods over those in sauces to control added sugars and preservatives.

- Select extra virgin olive oil for health benefits but use coconut or rapeseed oil for high-heat cooking. Avoid inflammatory vegetable and sunflower oils.

- For snacks, choose nuts, popcorn, and healthy toppings on crackers or rice cakes over crisps and highly processed snacks.

- Choose oats or homemade low-sugar muesli over sugary cereals for breakfast and avoid breakfast bars due to high sugar content.

- Treat chocolate, sweets, and biscuits as indulgences, and select high-quality options with fewer additives and better nutritional value.

- Frozen fruits and vegetables retain nutrients well, but most of the time don't have the texture and crunch of fresh fruits and vegetables. Make homemade meals over frozen ready meals to avoid additives.

- Support local artisans for higher quality, sustainable food, and foster a closer connection to the source of your food.

CHAPTER 21
FOOD LABELS

Understanding food labels can be tricky. It takes time and practice. Start at home by getting familiar with labels on the foods you eat regularly. Then when you are shopping, compare labels of similar products to find the healthiest option but be aware of a few sneaky tricks used to make food products seem healthier than they really are.

Nutrition information can be found on the back/side of food labels. Sometimes you will also find a snapshot of this information on the front of pack. Nutrition information is displayed per 100g and sometimes per recommended serving always be realistic yourself as to how much you're going to consume as a portion.

Some labels use colour coding to show, at a glance if a food is high, medium or low in fat, saturated fat, sugar and salt. Low (green) - the best choice, Medium (amber) - okay most of the time, High (red) - only choose occasionally.

I always use the per 100g column to compare products. Look at the recommended portion size. This may be far less than what you actually eat. For example a frozen pizza may say 4 portions per pizza and have a relatively reasonable traffic light score, but you have to ask yourself how you would feel about the score should it be doubled or even quadrupled.

The below table is roughly what the colour coded guidance is based on per portion:

	Low (green)	Medium (amber)	High (red)
Fat	3g or less	Between 3g and 17.5g	Over 17.5g
Saturated fat	1.5g or less	Between 1.5g and 5g	Over 5g
Sugars	5g or less	Between 5g and 22.5g	Over 22.5g
Salt	0.3g or less	Between 0.3g and 1.5g<	Over 1.5g

Nutrition claims

Some products claim to be 'low in fat' or a 'source of fibre' – but these claims don't mean the food is the healthiest option. It is best to look at all nutrients before making a decision. Some yogurts and dairy drink products need particular attention when it comes to making health claims. Recently I seen a fruit yogurt product that explicitly stated; "no added sugar" and "good for your gut". When I checked the label there was over 4 teaspoons of sugar per 125g portion. This is a prime example of how health claims can be deceiving most consumers of this product would consider the purchase to be a healthy food decision. The sugar was from the fruit source so "no added sugar" was correct but the product could never claim to be "low in sugar".

Ingredients List

By law, food manufacturers are required to list all ingredients in descending order by weight. This means that the first ingredient listed contributes the most by weight to the product, and the last ingredient the least. This ordering provides insight into the product's nutritional value and helps identify the predominant components, be they beneficial (such as whole grains in bread) or potentially harmful (such as sugar in a breakfast cereal).

The Quantitative Ingredient Declaration (QUID) provides the percentage of certain key ingredients, often seen in foods where the quantity of an ingredient is highlighted in the product's name or is particularly significant to the consumer. For instance, a "strawberry yogurt" must specify what percentage of it is actual strawberry. The QUID offers an additional layer of detail that can help consumers understand exactly what they are buying and consuming.

Encountering unrecognisable items on an ingredients list may be a red flag that the food is ultra-processed. Ultra-processed foods are not only far removed from their natural state but are also typically loaded with additives designed to enhance flavour, texture, or shelf life. Such foods may offer convenience but often at the expense of nutritional quality and health.

A good rule of thumb for evaluating the quality of a food product is to consider whether its ingredients are items you'd typically find in your kitchen and use in your cooking. Foods whose ingredients are whole and recognisable are generally preferable to those made from substances that sound more at home in a chemistry lab than in your kitchen pantry. Ingredients that you can easily identify are often a sign of minimal processing.

Artificial flavours, sweeteners, emulsifiers, and stabilisers are common in processed foods, but their impact on health, especially gut health, can be concerning. These substances can disrupt the delicate balance of gut bacteria, essential for digestion, immunity, and overall well-being. There's growing evidence that these additives may contribute to digestive issues and potentially other health problems over time.

Calories

Kilojoules and kilocalories measure the energy food provides to your body. 1 kcal is equivalent to 4.184 kj. Food energy might be listed in both units. Realistically Kcal is the one most people look for and refer to this simply as the calories within a product.

Your daily energy needs depend on various factors including age, sex, weight, height, and physical activity level. An average adult woman might need about 2,000 kcal per day, while an average adult man might need about 2,500 kcal. However, these needs will significantly vary based on age, height, weight and whether you are active or sedentary.

In my opinion the source of calories (whether from carbohydrates, proteins, fats, or sugars) matters more for your overall health. For example, calories from whole foods like fruits and vegetables come with essential nutrients and fibre, while calories from processed foods with added sugars may offer little nutritional value and can contribute to weight gain and other health issues.

Fat and "of which saturates".

It's possible to tell from your nutrition label how much saturate fat is in your packaged food and always aim for less than 1.5g per 100g. Anything over 5g per 100g is high in saturated fat and should be considered an indulgence.
Look for foods that are lower in total fat and particularly low in saturated fats. However, remember that some fats, like those found in nuts, seeds, avocados, and fish, are beneficial. It's the type of fat (e.g., omega-3 fatty acids) that matters. While saturated fats should be avoided if its from a single source (such as milk to produce butter) it far more preferential to a highly processed food that contains many ingredients you never heard of.

Carbohydrates and 'of which sugars'

Carbohydrate is made up of sugars, fibre, and starch. Your back of pack label will tell you the total amount of carbohydrate, and then it will break it down into 'of which sugars', highlighting the total content of sugars.

An unsweetened or unflavoured Greek yogurt may contain 6g total sugars - this is not added sugar, because when you check the ingredient list, it says: Ingredients: skimmed milk, cultures. Therefore, no sugar has been added, so you can deduce that this 6g of sugar is intrinsic sugar. Milk's primary intrinsic sugar is lactose.

Individual portions of fresh fruit salad may contain 10-15g of total sugars, all of which are naturally present within the cellular structure of the fruit (rather than added).

This means that food containing fruit or milk may be labelled amber or red. That's where you need to scan the ingredients to tell if the food contains added sugars. If it does not, this can be considered intrinsic sugar. Intrinsic sugar is not the priority when reducing your sugar intake. Added sugar is. Therefore, concentrate on removing products like fizzy drinks / sugar-sweetened beverages, sweets, jellies, cakes, biscuits, breakfast cereals, sweetened coffees, and sugar added to teas.

Sugars can be analysed from the carbohydrate 'of which sugars' section of your food label, but sweeteners may not. They are generally energy free, and therefore will only appear on the ingredients list. While sweeteners are a helpful substitute for sugar as part of a calorie-controlled diet, or for diabetics looking to balance their blood sugar, sweeteners can often provide up to 1000 times per gram the 'sweetness' detected by the taste buds and continue or even exaggerate a dependency on that sweet taste.

I've seen many variations of names for sugars hidden on labels, but you will always find these sneakily hidden under the section that says "carbohydrates, of which sugars". The sugar content will be zero or minimal, but the manufacturer will list these as other words like Dextrose, Fructose, Galactose, Glucose, Lactose, Maltose etc. In the ingredient list you may find lower calorie sweeteners such as sorbitol (produced from glucose), xylitol (from xylose), erythritol (from erythrose), lactitol (from lactose), maltitol (from maltose) etc. Remember the golden rule that the more processed your food is the worse it is for you so maybe a little sugar in its whole form is preferential to some sugar derived sweetener in these cases. Sweeteners cannot be broken down by the digestive system and may cause laxative effects if eaten in significant amounts.

Salt

Salt is composed of sodium chloride. Sometimes, food labels only give the figure for sodium, and the figure is in mg instead of g.

Salt labelling is mandatory in Ireland and is always expressed as 'salt'. Some products, however, especially if imported, may sometimes be written as 'sodium'. Adults should eat no more than the maximum of 6g of salt a day – that's around one teaspoon for the entire day. As this is an upper limit, not a target to reach, the lower you fall below that, the better. Salt figures on all packaging appear as grams.

Excessive salt intake can lead to high blood pressure, increasing the risk of heart disease and stroke. It can also cause kidney damage, osteoporosis, and fluid retention, exacerbating conditions like heart failure and leading to other health complications. So, it's important to be aware of your consumption.

Fibre

However, it's important to aim for over 30g of fibre daily. Population studies show most people consume only half that amount. For packaged foods, aim for a minimum of 6g of fibre per 100g serving. These studies also indicate that those following a Western diet, such as in Ireland, typically have no issues consuming enough protein but often lack sufficient fibre. Many people focus on protein intake, often considering it the key nutrient to monitor but as ive stated in an earlier chapter in more detail, fibre should be the number one nutrient to try to consume in all your meals. There is no upper limit to fibre consumption, provided it is introduced gradually.

Serving Sizes

Manufacturers can avoid sticking red traffic lights on their packaged goods by manipulating the serving size or portion size. Always check for what they have highlighted as a serving size and make sure it relates to what you plan to consume. A 500ml bottle of fizzy drink or 53g bar of chocolate may say there is 2 servings per package but realistically they will be consumed by one person, mostly in a single sitting. Be very aware of how the product will realistically be consumed.

353 Rule

While researching this area I came across the 353 rule which states, when purchasing any packaged foods, use the +353 rule as your threshold. That means if a product is over 3g of fat per 100g, over 5g of sugar per 100g and over 0.3g of sodium per 100g, it moves into amber or red traffic light, and will not be an ideal product to consume. As +353 is the international telephone dialling code for Ireland it is an easy one to remember.

Chapter Summary & Key Points

- Nutrition information is typically provided per 100g and per serving, but serving sizes can be misleading. Be aware of what your realistic serving size is and work off that.

- Color-coded labels help identify foods' nutritional value at a glance but may demonise fats from healthy sources or calories over ultra processed ingredients.

- Nutrition claims like "low in fat" don't necessarily mean a product is the healthiest choice, as seen in products with deceptive health claims.

- Ingredients are listed in descending order by weight, offering insights into a product's composition. The presence of unfamiliar or numerous ingredients may indicate a highly processed food.

- Prioritise an ingredient list of whole foods that you recognise every ingredient over calories and fat content.

- Learn to cook. Eat less processed food, eat more veg. Vegetables don't need an ingredient list or to make health claims.

CHAPTER 22
A ROUGH GUIDE TO EATING OVER A "NORMAL" WEEK

The simple choice of making good food decisions is essential for maintaining a healthy diet and overall well-being. The psychology behind these decisions, particularly in the morning, plays a significant role in shaping your choices throughout the day. Starting your day with a nutritious breakfast sets a positive tone for your eating habits. If you have no time for breakfast grab a piece of fruit on the way out the door. This is often referred to as the "halo effect," suggests that an initial good choice can lead to a series of subsequent good choices. A healthy breakfast can stabilise blood sugar levels, provide essential nutrients, and prevent excessive hunger later in the day. This not only supports physical health but also promotes mental clarity and focus, making it easier to stick to a balanced diet.

The psychology behind this is linked to the concept of decision fatigue. Our ability to make good decisions diminishes as we make more choices throughout the day. By starting with a healthy meal, you reduce the likelihood of choosing less nutritious options later, as your body and mind are already aligned with good food choices.

On the other hand, if you skip breakfast or start the day with an indulgent, high-sugar food item, you're more likely to experience blood sugar spikes and crashes. This can lead to increased cravings for unhealthy foods and a feeling of sluggishness, making it harder to resist temptation. The "what-the-hell" effect (a common psychological occurrence) may come into play here. If your first food choice of the day is poor, you might think, "I've already messed up today, I might as well indulge and start fresh tomorrow." This mindset often leads to a cascade of poor food choices, perpetuating an unhealthy cycle.

Hunger can significantly impair decision-making abilities. If you haven't eaten and find yourself hungry in a situation where indulgent foods are readily available, the physiological drive to satisfy immediate hunger can override long-term health goals. This is why it's crucial to plan and have healthy options available, reducing the risk of making poor choices when hunger strikes. This is why I try to grab a piece of fruit first thing in the morning, during the week, to consume on my commute to work. There is nothing nutritionally special about eating fruit first thing in the morning, but it's convenient, requires no preparation and that first food decision is made at the start of the day.

Breakfast

The ideal time to have breakfast can vary significantly from person to person, making it difficult to pinpoint a universally "best" time to break your fast. Factors such as individual metabolism, daily schedule, lifestyle, and personal preference all play a role in determining when someone should eat their first meal of the day. Therefore, while the timing of breakfast may differ, the emphasis should be on the quality and composition of the foods consumed when making your first food decision of the day.

For some, eating breakfast shortly after waking up works best. These individuals might find that an early breakfast helps kickstart their metabolism and provides the necessary energy to begin their day. This approach is particularly common among those who engage in early morning physical activity or have a physically demanding job.

Others might prefer to wait a few hours after waking before having breakfast. This could be due to personal preference, a later schedule, or practices like intermittent fasting. Intermittent fasting, for example, often involves extending the overnight fast until late morning or early afternoon. Research suggests that intermittent fasting can have various health benefits, such as improved metabolic health and weight management, but its effectiveness can vary between individuals.

Traditional breakfasts such as cereal or toast are not the ideal choices for a variety of reasons. These foods are often high in refined carbohydrates and sugars, leading to rapid spikes and subsequent crashes in blood sugar levels. This can leave you feeling hungry, tired, and unfocused shortly after eating. Instead, focusing on a breakfast rich in high-quality proteins, healthy fats, and plenty of fruits and vegetables provides sustained energy, stabilises blood sugar levels, and supports overall health. Proteins help to keep you full and satiated, while healthy fats support brain function and nutrient absorption. Including a variety of fruits and vegetables ensures you get a broad spectrum of vitamins, minerals, and antioxidants to kickstart your day.

Lunch

The perfect nutritional lunch on the run can vary depending on individual preferences and dietary needs, but there are a few key common principles to keep in mind to ensure that your lunch is both convenient and nutritious.

In colder weather, soups are an excellent choice. They can be packed with a variety of vegetables, providing a substantial number of vitamins, minerals, and fibre. A well-prepared soup often includes ingredients such as carrots, celery, tomatoes, leafy greens, all of which contribute to a nutrient-dense meal. Additionally, the warmth of the soup can be comforting and nourishing during the colder months, making it an ideal option for maintaining energy levels and overall well-being. Miso soups and broths are great choices also as they fill you up, are nourishing but are not too heavy causing you to feel sluggish afterwards.

When it comes to quick and easy lunches, a salad box is often a better option than a sandwich. One of the main reasons for this is the removal of highly processed bread, which is commonly used in sandwiches. Processed bread can be high in refined carbohydrates and added sugars, which can lead to rapid spikes and crashes in blood sugar levels, leaving you feeling tired and hungry soon after eating. By making or buying a salad box, you can fill your meal with a diverse variety of nutrient-dense foods. A well-composed salad can include a variety of fresh vegetables such as leafy greens, tomatoes, cucumbers, peppers, and carrots. Adding sources of protein like grilled chicken, tofu, beans, or chickpeas can help keep you full and satisfied. Healthy fats from ingredients like avocados, nuts, seeds, and olive oil not only enhance the flavour but also support brain function and nutrient absorption. Its best to avoid mayo-based salads in these boxes or at least keep them to a minimum. These salad boxes provide a high amount of dietary fibre, which is essential for digestive health and maintaining steady energy levels throughout the day.

Snacking through the day

When it comes to snacks on the go, fresh fruit and nuts are great choices for maintaining satiety and supporting overall health. These foods provide a balance of nutrients that help keep hunger at bay while offering various health benefits.

Fresh fruit is a fantastic snack option due to its natural sweetness, high water content, and rich nutrient profile. Fruits are packed with vitamins, minerals, and antioxidants that support immune function, skin health, and overall well-being. Additionally, the fibre in fruit helps slow down digestion, leading to a gradual release of energy and a prolonged feeling of fullness. The natural sugars in fruit provide a quick energy boost without the sharp spikes and crashes associated with refined sugars.

Nuts are a fantastic source of nutrition. They are rich in healthy fats, protein, and fibre, all of which contribute to feeling full after eating. The healthy fats in nuts, such as monounsaturated and polyunsaturated fats, support heart health and help to keep you feeling full for longer periods. Protein in nuts aids in muscle repair and maintenance, while fibre promotes digestive health and regulates blood sugar levels. The combination of these nutrients makes nuts a satisfying snack that can help curb hunger and prevent overeating later in the day.

Both fresh fruit and nuts are convenient and portable. They do not require refrigeration, can be easily packed into a bag, and can be consumed quickly and effortlessly. This convenience ensures that you have access to healthy snack options, even when you are on the move. For example, pairing an apple with a handful of almonds provides a satisfying and balanced snack. The apple offers a good dose of fibre and vitamins, while the almonds contribute healthy fats and protein. Similarly, combining berries with walnuts or a banana with a few cashews in a yogurt bowl creates a nutritious and filling snack that can help sustain energy levels throughout the day.

Dinner

The perfect nutritional dinner should be a well-balanced meal that incorporates a variety of food groups, focusing on plenty of exciting, flavoured vegetables, and whole grains. It's important to choose your vegetable elements first and base your proteins around them, as most people consuming a Western diet typically get sufficient protein, but we prioritise the protein (like chicken, steak, or fish) and starchy carbohydrates (like rice, pasta or potatoes) first then think of what vegetables to accompany after.

A nutritionally balanced dinner includes a diverse range of colourful vegetables. The more diverse the vegetables the more they provide different types of essential vitamins, minerals, and fibre, which are crucial for maintaining overall health and supporting digestive function. Whole grains, such as brown rice, quinoa, and whole-wheat pasta, should also be a staple. These grains are rich in fibre, help regulate blood sugar levels, and provide sustained energy.

Incorporating meat-free dinner meals can be both exciting and beneficial. Curries, for example, can be packed with vegetables, legumes, and aromatic spices, providing a hearty and flavourful meal. Italian dishes, such as vegetable-based dishes served with a little pasta or risotto, offer a great way to include a variety of vegetables and whole grains. Mexican cuisine, with its vibrant salads, bean-based dishes, and salsas, offers a variety of flavours and nutrients. Asian dishes often emphasise vegetables, tofu, and whole grains, making them perfect for a nutritious and balanced meal. These meals can be made delicious and appealing for children, helping them develop a taste for a variety of healthy foods from a young age.

Eating dinner as a family or group is equally important. It creates an opportunity for connection, conversation, and bonding. This shared time can encourage healthier eating habits, as meals are more likely to be balanced and thoughtfully prepared. Children who regularly eat with their families are more likely to consume fruits, vegetables, and whole grains, and less likely to eat unhealthy snacks. Family meals also provide a setting for parents to model healthy eating behaviours and engage children in meal preparation, which can increase their interest in nutritious foods.

Preparing meals around children is particularly important. Involving them in cooking can teach them about different foods, how they are prepared, and the benefits of a balanced diet. It can also make them more likely to try and enjoy new foods. Creating a positive mealtime environment helps establish lifelong healthy eating habits and can reduce picky eating behaviours.

Cup of tea

The Irish tradition of enjoying a cup of tea after dinner is a practised by all ages and demographics. This custom can also have beneficial effects on digestion. The warmth of the tea can help to soothe the digestive tract, promote gastric mobility, and assist in breaking down food more efficiently. Additionally, the ritual of drinking tea can signal to the body that it is time to unwind, helping to reduce stress and improve overall digestion.

While the traditional Lyons or Barry's black tea is a staple, incorporating herbal teas can offer various health benefits. Herbal teas such as peppermint, chamomile, and ginger are particularly effective for digestion. Peppermint tea can alleviate bloating and discomfort, chamomile tea is known for its calming properties, and ginger tea can help reduce nausea and stimulate digestive enzymes. Experimenting with different herbal teas can provide a gentle and natural way to support digestive health after a meal.

It is common to pair tea with biscuits or a sweet treat, but for those looking to make healthier choices, high cocoa dark chocolate paired with a handful of nuts is an excellent alternative. Dark chocolate, especially varieties with 70% cocoa or higher, is rich in antioxidants and can be beneficial for heart health. It also contains less sugar compared to typical sweet treats, making it a more nutritious option. Pairing dark chocolate with nuts such as almonds, walnuts, or hazelnuts not only adds a satisfying crunch but also provides additional health benefits. Nuts are a good source of healthy fats, protein, and various vitamins and minerals. They can help to keep you feeling full and provide sustained energy without the sugar crash associated with sugary snacks. The combination of dark chocolate and nuts can mimic the sensory experience of eating a biscuit.

Leave time to digest

Allowing your body sufficient time to digest meals and having a period of fasting can be highly beneficial for your overall health. Basically, this practice involves finishing dinner at a reasonable hour and avoiding snacking until the next morning.

When you give your body time to fully digest meals, it can function more efficiently. The digestive system needs a break to process the food, absorb nutrients, and clear out waste products. Eating late at night or snacking continuously can disrupt this natural process, leading to indigestion, poor sleep, and potential weight gain.

Fasting overnight, kind of like intermittent fasting, can also have positive effects on metabolism and weight management. By extending the period between your last meal and your next, your body can use stored energy more effectively, which can help in regulating blood sugar levels and promoting fat burning.

Eating dinner earlier and not snacking afterwards aligns with the body's natural circadian rhythms. Our bodies are programmed to be more efficient at processing food during the day, and late-night eating can interfere with this cycle, potentially affecting sleep quality and overall health.

Weekend

Eating at the weekend offers a great opportunity to enjoy indulgences while maintaining a healthy diet overall. If you eat an optimal diet 80% of the time, this leaves about four to five meals or snacks a week for indulgences. The weekend is logically the best time for these treats, as you have more opportunities to eat with friends and family. However, this doesn't mean every weekend meal should be an indulgence. Bolstering your healthy weekday eating by following the same healthy eating pattern during the weekend will help you feel better and see the results of your positive food choices.

When you do indulge, invest in the best form of your indulgences. For example, if you enjoy a cooked breakfast, try a brunch restaurant that specialises in this, or visit a local butcher to get the best quality sausages, black pudding, and thick-cut bacon. Alternatively, try different cooked breakfasts like eggs benedict, shakshuka, or avocado on sourdough with poached eggs and sriracha.

If you like fried chicken or burgers, avoid fast food or franchised establishments. Instead, seek out artisanal restaurants that serve tea-brined, buttermilk chicken or gourmet burgers. These food experiences may be more expensive but will be memorable and provide great topics for conversation with friends and family. Few people continue to discuss the pleasure of a particular fast-food meal after the fact.

For those who drink alcohol, the weekend or days off are preferred times to consume it, so the effects won't interfere with work. If you drink alcohol, ensure you eat well before and during consumption to slow the absorption of alcohol into the bloodstream. Hydrate with water before, during, and after drinking to avoid a hangover.

When dealing with a hangover, the goal is to rehydrate your body, replenish lost nutrients, and soothe your stomach. Water is crucial for hydration, so drink plenty to help your body recover. Electrolyte drinks like sports drinks, coconut water, or oral rehydration solutions can help replenish lost electrolytes. Bananas, high in potassium, help restore this important electrolyte. Eggs are packed with cysteine, an amino acid that helps break down acetaldehyde, a byproduct of alcohol metabolism. Simple carbohydrates like toast or crackers can help raise blood sugar levels without upsetting your stomach. Ginger tea can reduce nausea and settle your stomach. Porridge oats provide essential nutrients and helps stabilise blood sugar levels. Soups or broths, such as chicken noodle soup or miso soup, can help replenish sodium and other electrolytes. Honey contains fructose, which helps metabolise alcohol more quickly. Berries, high in antioxidants, can help reduce inflammation and oxidative stress caused by alcohol. Avocados are rich in healthy fats and potassium, which can help replenish lost nutrients. Asparagus contains amino acids and minerals that help protect liver cells and break down alcohol. Rest, hydration, and balanced nutrition are key to recovery. No matter how much you crave them avoid greasy or heavily processed foods, as they can exacerbate nausea and dehydration.

Once you follow these simple rules, you have the basic cornerstone of a healthy diet.

Chapter Summary & Key Points

- Starting the day with a nutritious breakfast can lead to better food choices throughout the day due to the "halo effect."

- Choosing high-sugar and starchy foods can cause blood sugar spikes, increased cravings, and lead to poor food choices later in the day.

- Planning and having healthy snacks available can prevent poor decision-making when hungry.

- Prioritising vegetables and whole grains in meals, along with family involvement, supports balanced nutrition and healthy eating habits.

- The weekend is a good time for indulgences if maintaining a healthy diet 80% of the time, and opting for high-quality indulgent foods can enhance enjoyment.

- Learn to cook. Eat less processed food and more fruits and vegetables.

CHAPTER 23
INDULGENCES

Remembering its ok to eat what you really crave and allowing indulgences occasionally is an important aspect of a balanced, healthy diet. It supports mental well-being and encourages a positive, mindful relationship with food. This mindset aligns with intuitive eating principles and can significantly benefit both your physical and mental well-being. When foods aren't off-limits, they become less tempting, and you're more likely to enjoy them in moderation. Regularly including your favourite foods in reasonable portions helps prevent the urge to overindulge and encourages a healthier relationship with all types of food.

Choosing your indulgences to a better standard is an excellent way to enjoy your favourite foods while maintaining a healthier and more balanced diet. By upgrading your indulgences, you can still satisfy your cravings without compromising on quality or nutritional value.

If your particular vice is a takeaway or fast-food burger, consider indulging in a gourmet burger at a quality restaurant instead. Gourmet burgers are often made with higher-quality ingredients, such as local beef, fresh vegetables, and artisanal buns. These burgers are not only more flavourful but also generally contain fewer additives and preservatives compared to fast food versions. By choosing a gourmet option, you can enjoy a more satisfying and nutritious meal.

If you love a fry-up at the weekend, try sourcing local, high-quality ingredients instead of relying on highly processed supermarket varieties. Look for local bacon and sausages from a trusted butcher and go for free-range eggs. These products often have better flavour and fewer additives. Supporting these local producers can provide fresher, more sustainable options.

If you're a fan of chocolate and sweets, consider choosing higher-quality options. Instead of mass-produced, cheap sweets and chocolates, go for chocolate from reputable brand or artisan producer that use minimal ingredients and higher cocoa content. Artisanal chocolates can provide a richer taste and often come with added health benefits due to the higher cocoa content. This way, you can indulge your sweet tooth without consuming excessive sugar and artificial additives.

If pizza is your indulgence, try making it at home with fresh, high-quality ingredients. Use whole grain or cauliflower crusts, fresh tomato sauce, and top it with a variety of vegetables and lean proteins. If you prefer dining out, choose an Italian restaurant or pizzeria known for using fresh, locally sourced ingredients and traditional cooking methods like Neapolitan style pizza. This upgrade ensures you enjoy a delicious pizza that's both satisfying and nutritionally superior to typical fast-food options.

If you love ice cream, consider treating yourself to artisanal or homemade versions. Artisanal ice creams often use higher-quality dairy, natural flavours, and fewer artificial ingredients. Alternatively, you can look up recipes and make your own at home using fresh fruit, natural sweeteners, and quality dairy or non-dairy alternatives. This approach allows you to indulge in a treat that is both delicious and better for your health.

By choosing your indulgences to a better standard, you can enjoy the foods you love while making healthier choices. This approach ensures that your treats are not only more satisfying but also less likely to derail your overall healthy eating plan. Upgrading your indulgences helps you maintain a balanced diet, supports local producers, and encourages mindful eating. It allows you to enjoy your favourite foods in a way that enhances both your physical and mental well-being.

Healthy eating is not an on/off switch.

When you restrict certain foods, it can create feelings of deprivation, guilt, and anxiety. By enjoying your favourite foods without guilt, you can foster a healthier, more positive relationship with what you eat. This approach reduces the risk of disordered eating patterns and enhances your mental health. What you're looking for is a sustainable eating pattern and one that you can stick to over the long term. Rigid diets with strict food rules are often hard to maintain. Allowing yourself to indulge occasionally makes it easier to stick to a healthy eating routine. When people feel deprived, they're more likely to overeat or binge when they finally give in to their cravings. If you don't consciously include indulgences in your diet, there's a risk that healthy eating can become an all-or-nothing mindset. This "on/off" approach can lead to several issues when you eventually do indulge in the foods you love.

When you view healthy eating as an "on/off" switch, any deviation from your strict diet can feel like a failure. This can lead to feelings of guilt and shame when you finally give in to a craving. Instead of enjoying the indulgence, you may find yourself overwhelmed with negative emotions, which can harm your mental health and your relationship with food. This mindset can lead to a dangerous cycle of bingeing and restriction. If you consider your indulgence as a complete derailment of your healthy eating plan, you might think, "I've already messed up, so I might as well keep eating poorly." This all-or-nothing thinking can result in overeating and a prolonged period of unhealthy eating, which undermines the progress you've made and can be damaging to your health.

On the other hand, when you intentionally choose your indulgences, you can enjoy them without guilt. Planning for indulgences means you're acknowledging that it's okay to enjoy all types of food in moderation. Probably my favourite indulgence meal is a gourmet burger with all the toppings washed down with a craft beer, or two so I have it occasionally when we eat out either with friends or as a family. This approach helps prevent the feeling of deprivation and makes it easier to return to your healthy eating habits after an indulgence.

Consciously allowing for indulgences also helps you maintain a positive and sustainable relationship with food. It reinforces the idea that healthy eating is about balance, not perfection. By integrating your favourite foods into your diet, you avoid the extremes of strict dieting and uncontrolled bingeing. This balanced approach makes it easier to stick to your healthy eating plan in the long term. When you plan for a treat, you can savour it fully, knowing that it's a part of your balanced diet. This mindful approach to eating helps you appreciate the food more and reduces the likelihood of overeating.

Balance

Nutritionally, it's all about balance, variety, and moderation. Enjoying a wide range of foods, including those you consider treats, ensures your diet is rich in different nutrients. Occasional treats won't negate the benefits of an otherwise healthy diet. It's crucial to focus on your overall eating habits rather than stressing over individual foods.
Eating within the pillars of a healthy diet for at least 80% of your meals is important for maintaining overall health and well-being. When you base this on around 21 meals per week, it means you have 16-17 meals that are nutritious and balanced, leaving 4-5 meals for indulgences.

Firstly, maintaining a healthy diet most of the time ensures that your body gets the essential nutrients it needs. These nutrients support vital bodily functions, boost your immune system, and help prevent chronic diseases such as heart disease, diabetes, and certain cancers. By eating healthily for most of your meals, you are doing enough to provide your body with a strong nutritional foundation.

Consistently eating nutritious foods helps regulate your metabolism and maintain a healthy weight. When you stick to a balanced diet for most of your meals, it's easier to manage your calorie intake and avoid the pitfalls of overeating. This balance can be more effective than restrictive diets, which often lead to cycles of deprivation and bingeing.

Eating healthily the majority of the time improves your energy levels and mental clarity. Nutritious foods provide the necessary fuel for your body and brain, helping you feel more energetic and focused throughout the day. When your diet is balanced, you're less likely to experience the energy crashes associated with consuming too many sugary or processed foods.

Saying that, allowing yourself around 4 meals for indulgences each week plays a crucial role in sustainably eating healthy and mental health. Indulgences can be a source of joy and satisfaction, and they help prevent feelings of deprivation that can lead to unhealthy eating patterns. Knowing you can enjoy your favourite foods occasionally makes it easier to stick to healthy eating habits in the long run. This flexible approach also encourages a healthier relationship with food. By not labelling foods as strictly "good" or "bad," you can enjoy a more balanced and less stressful eating experience. It helps reduce guilt and anxiety around food choices, fostering a more positive mindset towards eating.

Practising mindful eating is another key aspect. This means fully appreciating and enjoying the flavours, textures, and satisfaction your food provides. When you allow yourself to occasionally eat your favourite indulgences, you make sure you are taking time to savour and enjoy your food then you are making the eating experience more fulfilling, rather than mindlessly gorging on fast food in front of the TV or while scrolling on your phone.

Food Memories

Food indulgences often create lasting memories, especially when enjoyed with family and friends. Denying yourself these pleasures can lead to feelings of isolation or missing out on important social and cultural events. These experiences are not just about the food itself but also about the connections and joy of the event itself. It's important to embrace these moments, particularly with children, as they foster a positive relationship with food and create cherished memories, even if the food itself may not always be the healthiest.

A family BBQ is a great example of how food can bring people together. The smell of grilling meats, the sound of laughter, and the joy of eating outdoors all contribute to a memorable experience. For children, participating in a BBQ can be exciting and educational. They can learn about cooking, try new foods, and enjoy the company of family and friends. The menu may include indulgent items like burgers, hot dogs, and desserts, the overall experience is invaluable.

Enjoying ice cream on the beach is a classic summer activity that many children and adults look forward to. The combination of a sunny day, the sound of waves, and a cold frozen treat makes for a perfect memory. While ice cream may not be the healthiest option, its role in creating happy, carefree moments, especially for children is significant.

Regular family dinners, even if they occasionally include indulgent foods, are crucial for bonding and communication. Whether it's a Sunday roast, a pizza night, or a festive meal, these gatherings provide a space for family members to connect, share stories, and enjoy each other's company. For children, family dinners are an important part of their social development. They learn table manners, the importance of conversation, and the value of spending time together.

Creating these positive food memories with children helps them develop a healthy relationship with food. It teaches them that while nutritious eating is important, there is also a place for enjoyment and indulgence. These shared experiences reinforce family bonds and create traditions that can be passed down through generations. Whether it's the summer BBQ, the ice cream stand you visit every summer, or the special dishes prepared for family dinners, these rituals become part of a family's identity and heritage.

Indulging in alcohol

Indulging in alcohol can have significant consequences beyond the immediate effects of intoxication and a hangover. One of the less discussed but equally important dangers is how alcohol can lead to hedonistic eating, which often extends into the following days. Alcohol impairs judgment and lowers inhibitions, making it more likely that you will make poor food choices while drinking. This hedonistic eating typically involves high-calorie, high-fat, and high-sugar foods. The combination of alcohol and these foods can significantly increase your calorie intake, contributing to weight gain and poor nutrition.

When you are hungover, your body craves comfort foods to cope with the physical and emotional discomfort. These cravings are often for unhealthy, greasy, and sugary foods. The body's need for quick energy and the desire to alleviate nausea and fatigue drive these cravings. Consequently, a night of drinking can lead to a couple of days of poor eating habits, as you seek out these unhealthy comfort foods to feel better. Regular indulgence in alcohol can disrupt your overall eating patterns. The unhealthy eating that accompanies drinking and hangovers can interfere with your normal dietary routine, making it harder to return to balanced, nutritious meals. Over time, this can lead to chronic unhealthy eating habits and a decline in overall dietary quality.

Alcohol can negatively affect your metabolism and the way your body processes nutrients. It can interfere with the absorption of essential vitamins and minerals, leading to deficiencies that can affect your health in the long term. Additionally, the combination of alcohol and unhealthy food can strain your digestive system, leading to issues such as indigestion and gastrointestinal discomfort. The caloric content of alcohol combined with hedonistic eating can lead to significant weight gain over time. Excess weight is associated with a range of health issues, including cardiovascular disease, diabetes, and certain cancers. The empty calories from alcohol, coupled with the additional calories from unhealthy food, contribute to these risks.

Beyond the physical effects, there are psychological consequences to consider. Regular indulgence in alcohol and subsequent unhealthy eating can lead to symptoms of declining mental health. These negative emotions can further perpetuate a cycle of unhealthy behaviour, as individuals may turn to alcohol and comfort food as coping mechanisms. Additionally, the psychological effects and impact on sleep and energy levels further complicate efforts to maintain a balanced and healthy lifestyle.

Cook your indulgences yourself.

As I've mentioned before in this book, and I can't stress this enough, that the best way to indulge in the foods you love is to learn how to cook them from scratch. This approach offers numerous benefits, from full control over the ingredients to enhanced flavour, and it creates a positive cooking and eating environment for the whole family.

When you cook from scratch, you have complete control over the ingredients that go into your meals. This means you can choose high-quality, fresh, and nutritious ingredients, and avoid additives, preservatives, and excessive amounts of unhealthy fats, sugars, and salts often found in processed foods. This control allows you to make healthier versions of your favourite dishes with probably better flavour than industrial produced foods.

Homemade meals often taste better because you can tailor them to your personal preferences without using industrial ingredients, many of which contain chemicals within them you wouldn't nor shouldn't use at home. You can adjust seasonings, experiment with different herbs and spices, and use fresh ingredients that enhance the flavour of your dishes. The process of cooking itself can bring out the best in your ingredients, resulting in a more delicious and satisfying meal. Cooking from scratch helps you develop valuable culinary skills. Whether you're learning basic techniques like chopping and pan frying or more advanced methods like baking and grilling, these skills are useful and rewarding. As you become more proficient in the kitchen, you gain confidence and creativity, which can make cooking an enjoyable and fulfilling activity.

When you cook at home, you create an atmosphere where cooking and food positivity are embraced and enjoyed by the entire family. Cooking together can be a fun and bonding experience, whether it's preparing a weekend breakfast or a festive holiday meal. This communal activity can teach children the importance of healthy eating and cooking skills, setting them up for a lifetime of good habits. You can learn about different ingredients, where they come from, and their nutritional benefits. This knowledge can lead to more informed food choices and a deeper appreciation for what you eat. Additionally, involving children in cooking can teach them valuable lessons about nutrition, mathematics (through measuring and portioning), and science (through understanding how ingredients react during cooking).

Preparing your own meals encourages mindful eating. When you've invested time and effort into cooking a meal, you're more likely to savour and appreciate it. This mindfulness can lead to a greater awareness of hunger and fullness cues, helping to prevent overeating and promoting a healthier relationship with food.

Whether it's a weekly pizza night, a Sunday roast, or Christmas/ Easter baking sessions, these rituals become remembered parts of family life. These traditions help strengthen family bonds and create a sense of continuity and belonging. By embracing home cooking, you can create delicious, healthier meals while building lasting traditions and memories.

Chapter Summary & Key Points

- Allow indulgences as part of a balanced diet. Enjoying your favourite foods in moderation encourages sustainable healthy eating in the long term.

- Upgrade your indulgences by choosing higher-quality versions. If you're going to eat them less make sure your eating them in the best quality you can.

- Avoid viewing healthy eating as an on/off switch. Allowing occasional treats helps maintain a positive relationship with food.

- Food indulgences create lasting memories, especially when shared with family and friends. Embrace these moments and don't feel guilty about them.

- Learn to cook your indulgences from scratch. You will have control over ingredients. This approach supports healthier eating habits and family traditions.

- Eat less processed food and more fruits and vegetables. At least 80% of the time.

ABOUT THE AUTHOR

John Core, born and raised in Dublin, Ireland, has a rich background in culinary and catering operations. From a young age, he has worked in the world of professional cookery, working in a variety of hospitality settings, including hotels, restaurants, fine dining establishments, contract catering, and event catering. His diverse experience and dedication have earned him multiple awards in professional cookery, catering operations management, and culinary nutrition.

In 2020, John graduated from TU Dublin with an MSc in Applied Culinary Nutrition. This academic achievement has allowed him to specialise in culinary nutrition, focusing on promoting healthy eating habits through practical and accessible advice. Over the years, his career has taken him to professional kitchens across Europe, Australia, and America, where he has continually expanded his culinary knowledge.

His curiosity for all types of food, combined with his extensive experience and academic background, makes him a trusted voice in the field of culinary nutrition.

Currently, John resides in Wexford with his wife, Roisin, and their twin sons, Cillian and Aidan.

Printed in Great Britain
by Amazon